FOR SENIORS ONLY!

Student
WORKBOOK

Dudley Callison

FACE TO FACE MINISTRIES is a non-profit organization for college students in Waco, Texas. The vision of Face To Face is for students in this generation to encounter God in personal and profound ways. We are confident that a college student who knows God intimately will walk with Him for a lifetime.

Face To Face offers large and small group Bible study opportunities. Currently, Face To Face hosts TouchStone Bible Study, a weekly gathering of more than 1,000 college students representing most denominations and ministries in Waco. TouchStone provides a common ground for Christian students to stand together, touching the Father's heart in worship and standing on the solid rock of His Word.

Visit the Face To Face web site at:
http://www.baylor.edu/~face-to-face/
or E-mail us: facetoface@easy.com
P. O. Box 6335, Waco, TX 76706
254.753.2877

Visit the Cross Training Publishing web site at:
http://www.crosstrainingpub.com
Our contact information for product orders is:
1-800-430-8588

All Scripture quotations are taken from The Holy Bible, New International Version. Copyright 1973, 1978, 1984 by International Bible Society.
© 1998 Cross Training Publishing

For Seniors Only!

Requests for information should be addressed to:
Cross Training Publishing
P.O. Box 1541
Grand Island, NE 68802

ACKNOWLEDGMENTS

When the seniors from Tallowood Baptist Church in Houston didn't show up for summer-time youth functions, I went out looking for them. Little did I know it would lead to a series of discussions regarding this transition time in life. I can remember hearing them say they felt like they had been kicked out of the youth group, but not kicked quite hard enough to make it into the college group. They just didn't fit anymore. "We need something just for us. . .something that will answer the questions we are having about the future." To this group of frustrated students I say thanks. Thanks for moving me out of traditional methods of ministry to see your specific need. Thanks for letting me listen in as you tried to figure out what the future held, and who held the future. Thanks for placing your seedling questions in the soil of my heart where they could germinate for a season. God has used you to bring a harvest to many seniors who have asked the same things you did years ago.

As I write, my mind flashes pictures of the many people who contributed to this workbook.

- For my understanding of what it means to be in Christ, I thank Gary Stroope and Louie Giglio. No two men have been more instrumental in my spiritual formation.

- For offering wise counsel as I seek to follow God's leadership, I thank Will Cunningham, Dennis Perry, and Gary Swanson.

- For providing a home where I could understand God's love for me, I thank my wonderful parents and family.

- For contributing in special ways to this project, I thank Trent Henderson for his creative assistance, the leadership of Face To Face for their constant prayerful support, and Kylie Lindsey for serving as our text consultant. I owe a deep debt of gratitude to my editor, Kelley Smith, who transforms my normal words into something God can use. May this be the first of your many publications.

- For her ever loving devotion, I thank my sweet wife. The only thing to which I can compare God's grace is the undeserved love I have from you.

STARTING THE JOURNEY...

LET ME INTRODUCE YOU to a few people who have traveled this road before you. See if you know anyone like them.

First, meet Carol. She was a member of the youth council at church. She had it all together. In fact, one week at Wednesday night Bible study, she and a friend stood up and quoted the entire Sermon on the Mount from memory! But after one year at the university, you could not distinguish Carol from the most non-Christian student on campus. She had it spiritually, then lost it all.

Then meet Brad. He enjoyed church in high school, except for the fact that his parents made him go to everything. As high school graduation neared, his parents suddenly became more strict. They made statements like, "As long as you're under this roof, you're under these rules!" Finally Brad moved to his own place and started a new job. No more "roof" meant no more rules. Each Sunday he felt like he probably should get up for church, but before long, sleeping in became normal. . .then Brad didn't worry about church anymore.

Now meet Jill. She went to church because it was a pretty good time. She liked the youth minister and the activities he planned. Since most of her best friends were in the youth group, church was comfortable, safe place. After moving away to college, she began visiting other churches, but she hated being a "visitor." No church was like her home church. Finally, not wanting to feel awkward anymore, she just decided to go home when she could.

Lastly, meet Tim. He went through the typical ups and downs of the Christian life through high school. Along the way, Tim began having a Quiet Time. It was difficult at first, but he began to look forward to those private moments with God. When Tim moved away from home it took some time to find a new church, but his growth never stopped. He had learned how to grow on his own. After a year, Tim realized he was actually closer to God than he had been in high school.

Do any of these stories sound familiar? Not only are they all true, the same stories repeat themselves all the time. You may be wondering why you read about three bad endings and only one good ending. Well, that reflects how many high school Christians actually continue the spiritual journey after leaving home. That means among you and three of your friends, only one of you is likely to stay on course after high school.

So what is it going to take for you to keep growing spiritually after you graduate? You must learn how to feed yourself. Consider this illustration: What if you decided to eat out

every meal, but you only had enough money to go to restaurants twice a week. You might go to some "All You Can Stomach" buffet to really load up for Sunday lunch and try to make it to Wednesday supper for your next meal. When Wednesday rolled around, you would go out and gorge again, hoping you had taken in enough calories to make it all the way to the next Sunday. What a crazy way to live!

If it is crazy to live this way physically, why do so many Christians try to live this way spiritually? We all have spiritual hunger. Yet many believers in high school try to settle for two "feedings" per week. . .Sunday and Wednesday. So what happens spiritually between meals? One reason high school Christians discontinue the spiritual journey after leaving home is that they have never learned the keys to spiritual fitness. By not taking in spiritual nourishment on their own, they eventually starve. Too many students have learned how to eat what the church offers, but have not learned how to feed themselves.

This workbook is about continuing your spiritual journey. To stay healthy along the road, you must learn to nourish yourself. The daily studies are designed to give you practical tools for spiritual growth. You will consider post-high school, real life situations that only the spiritually strong can survive. Each week you will work through five Bible studies on your own—just you and the Holy Spirit applying Scripture that will nourish your faith. Do your best to keep up with the daily studies. If you try to "swallow" three days at once, you will get behind and miss the point of this study altogether. Hopefully you will learn how to sit down at the banquet table with God and walk away spiritually satisfied.

A WORD OF CAUTION!!! This study is not for lightweights. It starts off with two assumptions: You are smart enough to learn on your own, and you really do want to survive spiritually after you leave home. Remember, many intend to grow in faith after high school, but only a few really do. Join the growing ranks of those who continue the journey.

Let's get started. . .

CONTENTS

WEEK 1

Social Security

Week One:

SOCIAL SECURITY

A college freshman walked nervously into the first day of statistics class. So many students failed this course that upperclassmen jokingly referred to it as "sadistics." Not one to let intimidation get the best of her, the freshman spent the summer months reviewing everything from algebra to calculus. An anxious hush fell over the room as the professor stepped in to deliver his first lecture of the new semester. He announced, "Today we will review the principles of adding, subtracting, multiplying, and dividing." What?! She couldn't believe her ears. Was the professor really going to review basic mathematics? He did. All hour he covered the fundamentals. A bit frustrated at the elementary nature of the lecture, the freshman strode up to the professor and said, "I heard this class was really tough. Why did you waste our time on basic math?" He replied, "The answer is simple." "If you don't understand what we covered today, you will never pass this class in the end. All of complex statistics hinges on these basic principles."

Your ability to continue the spiritual journey after high school does not depend on reviewing Scripture memory or maintaining church attendance. Rather, it depends on your understanding and applying the most fundamental truth of the Christian life: Your identity is in Christ. This phrase, in Christ, may be so overused in Your experience that you feel like moving on to a more complex spiritual subject. But don't rush ahead! Everything you will study in the remaining seven weeks hinges on your understanding the truth in this first week. A Chinese proverb says, "The journey of a thousand miles begins with a single step." Your destination in life may be too far away to see, but if you look back at your journey, you will see that your first steps clearly read, "in Christ." Everything else is down the road.

Day 1 Changing Times
Day 2 In Christ
Day 3 Free at Last
Day 4 Real Life
Day 5 More Real Life

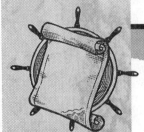

MEMORY VERSE FOR THE WEEK:

Ephesians 1:11-12
In him we were also chosen, having been predestined according to the plan of him who works out everything in conformity with the purpose of his will, in order that we, who were the first to hope in Christ, might be for the praise of his glory.

DAY 1: CHANGING TIMES

Graduation from high school looms near—an event you've anticipated for a lifetime. Ironically, the only thing you can count on for sure is that things are going to change. Whether you are prepared or not, you are about to go through a major transformation in life. Almost everything that gives you security will alter in some way.

Of course, the idea of change is bittersweet. Change has the potential to wreak havoc in your life or to bring happiness you've never before experienced. Some of the change is good; some of it may not be so pleasant. Either way, change is inevitable, and this transition time after high school is vital as God continues to bring you through change to make you into the image of Jesus.

But before you consider who you will become in life, take a look at who you have been in high school.

Answer the following questions with words or phrases that describe yourself over the past few years. Answer honestly, according to who you really *are*, not necessarily who you might *like* to be.

How do you see yourself academically in high school?
(good, lazy, driven, externally motivated, procrastinator, . . .)

How have you been socially?
(active, leader, removed, nonexistent, frustrated, . . .)

How do you feel athletically?
(varsity, closet, indifferent, couch potato, stud, spectator, . . .)

How do you see yourself spiritually?
(growing, active, mediocre, stale, passionate, roller coaster, . . .)

Which of the above areas do you hope changes the most after high school?

Which of the above areas do you hope changes the least after high school?

Change is inevitable.

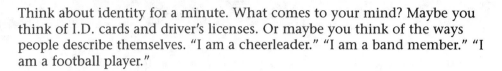

Think about identity for a minute. What comes to your mind? Maybe you think of I.D. cards and driver's licenses. Or maybe you think of the ways people describe themselves. "I am a cheerleader." "I am a band member." "I am a football player."

These activities identify certain students. In high school, it is easy to designate people according to what they do; it is easy to mistake *identity* with *activity* because people tend to act according to who they think they are. In reality, these labels describe behavior more than identity.

Another tendency is for students to be identified by social groups, the people they hang out with. Think about the groups at your school. Write down some of the social groups in the box below.

Preps? Kickers? Jocks? Brains? Goths? How did they get those labels? Well, that's what they do, and that's who they hang out with. Kickers wear boots and drive pickups. Jocks play sports and earn varsity letters. Preps wear denim and khakis. Party-ers drink and go clubbing. Goths wear black and listen to alternative music. You get the picture.

Finding your identity in what you do or who you hang out with means trouble. You will undoubtedly experience an identity crisis when you finish high school and move to the next season of your life, whether it be college, a job, or some other opportunity.

Basing your identity on what you do is dangerous because activities change. Jocks aren't always the stars on the football team after high school. Party-ers aren't known at college for the great beer bash they had last January, because nobody at college was at that party, or really cares. Most band members don't become drum majors, and Student Council will elect new officers.

Those things which provided security and identity in high school no longer support you. This upheaval may cause you to grasp for a new source of identity. Some try Greek organizations; others look to dating relationships or other sources of stability. Here, the problem remains—you will still be defining yourself by *what you do* and *who you hang out with*.

If you base your identity in your activities, graduating will be like losing your driver's license—or your I.D. card. If you enroll in college, this truth will become evident to you the first time you lose your I.D. card. Hopefully, this will not be too common of an event for you! You quickly learn how important your I.D. is when you realize you can't eat lunch in the cafeteria, you can't sign up for intramural sports, you can't go to the library (assuming you'd *want* to!), you can't go to the gym to exercise, and you miss the athletic events. All because you've lost the card which identifies you as a student.

You see, when you lose your identity, you lose your security. The scary part about graduating from high school is that you have the potential to lose another kind of I.D.—the one that defines who you are in Christ. And you need this identity to determine how to handle situations in life. When your identity is securely fixed in Christ, you will be able to respond to the new circumstances you will encounter when you leave home. You can say, "I know what to do because I know who I am."

Write Hebrews 13:8 in the blanks below:

_____

_____

When other people and circumstances change, Jesus remains the same. God has designed you with a new, stable identity. He has made you to be a new creation; you are now *in Christ*. Being *in Christ* has some vital implications for you.

During the next few days, you will explore more fully what being *in Christ* means. You will have the opportunity to examine how your identity in Christ will form the framework in which you can expect to make godly choices now and for the rest of your life.

Many high school Christians drop out of the spiritual race after leaving home for this reason: They lose sight of their identity in Christ and try to find stability in other places. Will you now choose to stay in the race?

DAY 1 SUMMARY

- Life's about to change.
- The only stable identity is in Christ.

Make this your prayer today:

Dear Lord, you are the same yesterday, today, and always. Help me to look to you alone for identity and security. Even though my circumstances are about to change, I pray that my faith in you will grow stronger. Show me who I am in Christ. In days to come, I want to. . .

(Finish your prayer here.)

_____

_____

_____

_____

_____

When your identity changes, you lose your security.

You find stable identity in Christ.

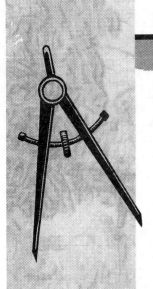

DAY 2: IN CHRIST

As you explored in the previous session, when a loss of identity occurs, you may try to re-establish it again *somewhere* else, or in *someone* else. Upon leaving high school, most students will grope and search for new friends, a club or social group, a dating relationship. . .something that will help define "This is who I am now." The only eternally stable way to identify yourself is in Christ.

So, what does it mean to be *in Christ?* It might be hard to grasp this theological concept. It may be easier to understand what it means to be *in Christ* when you compare it to some of the other things you are in. Being in a family, for instance, usually means you live with other family members while you are young; you eat meals together, travel together, support one another, etc.

Describe what it means for you to be in the following:

school:

_____

_____

a dating relationship:

_____

_____

an organization:

_____

_____

church:

_____

_____

Being *in* school means you go to class every day, complete homework assignments, and look forward to a few months off during the summer. If you are *in* a dating relationship, you spend a lot of time with another person. Dating may mean long phone conversations, plans on Valentine's

Day, and occasional gifts for each other. Being *in* an organization means wearing the T-shirt, going to meetings, being identified with others in the group, and having a sense of belonging. Membership *in* church means being a part of a church family and worshipping on Sundays; it may also mean getting the newsletter, going on retreats and to camp.

All these things give you a sense of belonging, a sense ownership and pride. Membership is something we all crave—and need.

The Bible speaks very clearly about what it means to have membership *in Christ*. In fact, the New Testament uses the phrase *in Christ* 89 times! Read the following Scripture passages, writing down what each says about who you are in Christ. Use the first one as an example for how to do the rest.

Romans 8:1-2
Therefore, there is now no condemnation for those who are in Christ Jesus, because through Christ Jesus, the law of the Spirit of life set me free from the law of sin and death.

Being in Christ means *I am not condemned for my sin.*

Romans 8:38-39
Being in Christ means _____

Ephesians 4:32
Being in Christ means _____

Philippians 4:19
Being in Christ means _____

2 Corinthians 5:17
Being in Christ means _____

Next, read Ephesians 1:3-14 below. This passage is filled with affirmations of your identity in Christ. Circle the words that describe what God has done for you because you are *in Christ*. You should find about 13 of them.

Praise be to the God and Father of our Lord Jesus Christ, who has blessed us in the heavenly realms with every spiritual blessing in Christ. For he chose us in him before the creation of the world to be holy and blameless in his sight. In love he predestined us to be adopted as his sons through Jesus Christ, in accordance with his pleasure and will to the praise of his glorious grace, which he has freely given us in the One he loves. In him we have redemption through his blood, the forgiveness of sin, in accordance with the riches of God's grace that he lavished on us with all wisdom and understanding. And he made known to us the mystery of his will according to his good pleasure, which he purposed in Christ, to be put into effect when the times will have reached their fulfillment to bring all things in heaven and on earth together under one head, even Christ.

In him we were also chosen, having been predestined according to the plan of him who works out everything in conformity with the purpose of his will, in order that

You have membership in Christ.

we, who were the first to hope in Christ, might be for the praise of his glory. And you also were included in Christ when you heard the word of truth, the gospel of your salvation. Having believed, you were marked in him with a seal, the promised Holy Spirit, who is a deposit guaranteeing our inheritance until the redemption of those who are God's possession to the praise of his glory.

These Scripture passages are just a few examples, but the promises are sure. *In Christ*, you are not condemned; you are useful, fit for service, and valuable. God's love is inseparably linked to you. You are forgiven. You are provided for. You are blessed, chosen, adopted, redeemed, loved, and sealed with the Spirit.

Your identity in Christ is not just a theological concept; it applies to real life, helping you determine how to act in every situation. Remember (in Day One), you discovered that your behavior doesn't determine your identity. In fact, your identity determines your behavior. Let's take a practical look at how this works.

Read Colossians 3:5-10. Write in the lines below what actions/behaviors you must "put to death" or "put aside" since you are in Christ.

_____

_____

_____

Now, read Colossians 3:12-17. Write in the lines below what actions/behaviors you must "put on" since you are *in Christ*.

_____

_____

_____

As you can see, the behavior of those who are *in Christ* differs greatly from the behavior of those who are in the world. Since behavior naturally flows from identity, it is normal for people who are in the world to act lustful, angry, greedy, and immoral. In contrast, if you are in Christ, you naturally act as Jesus would—compassionate, kind, humble, and forgiving.

During the next three days, you will take time to explore how being in Christ relates to freedom and responsibility in real life situations.

DAY 2 SUMMARY

Being *in Christ* means you are intimately connected to the person of Christ; your behavior results from this identity.

Make this your prayer today:

*Dear Lord, thank you for giving me life in Christ. Thank you for giving me belonging, ownership, and security in you. Help me live in a way that reflects your life **in me**. I'm most thankful for these benefits of being in Christ:*

(Finish your prayer here.)

_____

_____

_____

_____

_____

_____

DAY 3: FREE AT LAST

Graduation from high school means you are **free at last**, right? No more curfews. No more of mom and dad's asking if you've finished your homework. No one saying you have to go to church—unless you want to go.

No doubt about it, freedom can be one of the greatest things about getting older. You get to make most of the decisions about your life, and no one really has much to say about it.

Freedom is an interesting paradox, though. Think about a baby. Babies spend a lot of time in play-pens or being cradled by their parents. Eventually, they learn to crawl. . .talk about freedom! Now they get to scoot all around the house, grabbing things they've never been able to reach.

Or think about when you first got your driver's license.

What new freedoms did you have?

```



```

And when you graduate from high school? What freedoms are you looking forward to the most?

```



```

With each growing step—from infancy to adolescence to adulthood—come new avenues of freedom, which in turn brings joy.

When a baby starts crawling, it gets to actually decide where to go next! There is a whole new world of things to be touched, smelled, and eaten! And a teenager getting a driver's license—wow! You can run over to friend's house, make a quick trip to McDonald's for some fries, and you don't have to call Mom or Dad for a ride home!

Graduating from high school ushers in the greatest step toward freedom in you life so far. You get to start with a clean slate. If you go away to college or get a new job with new employers and co-workers, they don't know about all your mistakes in high school. They don't remember the time you got locked in your locker your freshman year. No one asks about your SAT or ACT scores, or what clubs you were a member of. Perhaps you hope people will remember your accomplishments, or maybe you are looking forward to getting rid of the "ghosts" from your past. Either way, you are starting over.

This joy that freedom brings is a picture of what Christ did on the cross.

Write out Colossians 2:13b-14 in the blanks below.

_____

_____

_____

_____

What does this say about what Jesus did on the cross?

_____

_____

_____

_____

Jesus set you free from sin. When he died, he defeated the power sin has over your life. This means that when you became a Christian, God gave you a clean slate! You have freedom from your sin. Your past no longer determines your future.

But there is more to it. While Christ has given you freedom *from* sin, He has not given freedom *to* sin. This means that just because you know God forgives, you cannot go out and sin all you want. In Romans 6:15, Paul says it this way: "What shall we say then? Shall we go on sinning so that grace may increase? By no means! We died to sin. How can we live in it any longer?"

Read Galatians 5:13.

How does this Scripture say you should handle freedom?

_____

_____

You see, with the freedom from sin that Christ gives, He also requires responsibility. He has called you to walk righteously, to make moral, Christlike decisions.

It's the same way with the freedoms discussed earlier in this session. Consider the freedom you have with your driver's license—you can run errands by yourself and be your own chauffeur, but, as you know, with that freedom come several new responsibilities. You have to study the rules of the road. You have to learn your way around town. You have to obey the laws the government has set out for you and be careful of other drivers and pedestrians. Are you beginning to see the connection between freedom and responsibility?

Think about the responsibilities that will accompany the freedoms you will experience when you graduate from high school and leave home. If you go to college and live in the dorm, you probably won't have a curfew anymore. You will have the freedom not to go to bed at night; along with that freedom, though, comes the responsibility to get up for the class in the

In Christ, you are free from sin.

morning. Likewise, you *do* have the freedom to skip that class, but you have the responsibility to pass the class and to be a good steward of your education. After high school, you have the freedom to choose a job that will earn you money. Along with this freedom, though, you must take responsibility to show up for work, complete your job assignments, and keep from getting fired. With this job, you will have the freedom to decide what to do with the money you earn. Accordingly, you will have the responsibility of balancing your checkbook and thus avoiding bounced checks and bank fees.

Which of these new areas of freedom concerns you the most?

Each degree of freedom brings an equal degree of responsibility.

So you can see, responsibility and freedom are related. Responsibility affords you opportunity either to abuse your freedom or to walk righteously in it. With each degree of freedom comes an equal degree of responsibility. In order to fully enjoy the benefits of freedom in Christ, you must willingly shoulder the responsibility of Christian living.

To review a bit from the last two sessions, recall what happens when insecurity comes from losing your identity. This loss qualifies you as a candidate to abuse your new-found freedom after high school. For the last two days of this week, you will have an opportunity to apply these truths to real-life situations you may encounter during the transition after high school.

Take a moment to write out the memory verse for this week in the blanks below:
Ephesians 1:11-12

_____

_____

_____

DAY 3 SUMMARY

• Graduation from high school means freedom.
• Freedom brings joy and responsibility.
• In order to enjoy your freedom, you must bear the responsibility.

Make this your prayer today:

Dear Lord, thank you for the freedom you have given me through Jesus Christ. Help me not to abuse that freedom, but to use it to honor you. God, you know I desire freedom; give me the strength to be responsible. I lay these concerns before you:

_____

_____

_____

_____

DAY 4: REAL LIFE

The last two days of this week will help you draw together and apply the concepts you've been exploring so far. You have discovered that being *in Christ* is the only stable, lasting identity and that being *in Christ* means living a life that reflects His character in you.

As you learned earlier this week, loss of your identity can lead to loss of security, which can lead to abuse of freedom. This is why it is so important to understand your identity in Christ. This is independent of the activities and circumstances in your life; even when what you do every day changes, your identity in Christ remains the same. This stable and true identity allows you to make responsible and wise decisions when you are faced with new situations. You now make decisions based on the question, "What is the appropriate choice that reflects my identity in Christ?"

Read through the following scenarios (4 today and 4 tomorrow). For each scenario, you will explore the contrast between ungodly and godly responses in these circumstances. After each real-life situation, you will see passages of Scripture listed. Read each passage and follow the instructions below it.

1 You have just attempted to join a Greek organization at your new college. You were offered invitations by several groups, but not the one you really wanted. You feel turned down, upset, and most of all, rejected.

• **How would a non-Christian handle rejection?**

_____

_____

_____

God's
acceptance is
far more
valuable than
acceptance
from the
world.

Now read Ephesians 1:4.

Being *in Christ* gives you this confidence: Even though you may be rejected by people, you are chosen by God.

Now rewrite this as a personal statement:

I may be rejected, but in Christ _____

As a Christian, you can handle rejection from any source by refusing to respond sinfully and by looking to people God places in your life for companionship. Knowing that you are chosen by God gives you the strength to handle rejection righteously.

2 You realize that changing your major from Pre-Med to Education potentially cuts your salary by two-thirds. You may now be destined for a life of tight finances instead of luxury.

• **How would a non-Christian handle this change?**

_____

_____

_____

Now read Matthew 6:25-34.

Being *in Christ* gives you this confidence: Even though you may be poor in the eyes of the world, you will be provided for by the hand of God.

Rewrite this as a personal statement:

_____

_____

As a Christian, you can live without luxury because you know that Christ provides everything you need. In Christ, you can live without anxiety, finding contentment in all circumstances.

3 You chose a college or a workplace where you don't know anyone. Now the people you met during orientation or training want to go out and party. You are free from having your high school reputation to worry about, free from your parents' curfew, and you don't want to disappoint your new friends.

• How would a non-Christian handle this new freedom?

_____

_____

_____

Now read Galatians 5:1, 13 and 1 Peter 2:16.

Being *in Christ* gives you this confidence: Even though you are free to sin, you can choose to use your freedom to serve others.

Rewrite this as a personal statement:

_____

_____

As a Christian, God commands you to use your freedom to serve others and build His kingdom. Rather than focusing on your new friends' disappointment that you are not going out with them, you can serve them by offering positive alternatives where everyone can be accepted.

4 You and the person you've been dating have just broken up. You are very sad because you thought this might have been "the one." Your heart hurts, but the problem is that usually when you hurt you turn to him or her. Now you have no one. You feel lonely and desperate for companionship.

• **How would a non-Christian handle hurt and loneliness?**

_____

_____

_____

Now read Matthew 28:20, John 14:16-18, and Psalm 147:3.

Being *in Christ* gives you this confidence: Even though you may feel lonely, hurt, or abandoned, you can find companionship and healing in the presence of God.

Rewrite this as a personal statement:

_____

_____

Contentment is found in Christ.

God is your most constant friend.

As a Christian, you can handle loneliness by looking to God as your most constant friend. When the loss of a relationship occurs, your relationship with God will heal your broken heart.

DAY 4 SUMMARY

• Identity in Christ is not just a theory; it builds a framework from which you can make godly decisions in real life situations.

• Identity in Christ teaches you how to handle rejection, career decisions, freedom, and loneliness or hurt.

Make this your prayer today:

Dear Lord, when I am faced with these difficult situations in my life, help me recognize my identity in you and make godly choices based on it. Out of these situations I considered, I am most concerned about my ability to. . .

_____

_____

_____

_____

DAY 5: MORE REAL LIFE

Let's take a closer look at the memory verse for the week.
Ephesians 1:11-12

In him we are also chosen, having been predestined according to the plan of him who works out everything in conformity with the purpose of his will, *in order that we*, who were the first to hope in Christ, *might be for the praise of his glory.*

In the blanks below, write the body of the sentence, which is in italics:

_____

_____

Notice the reason for which God chose us to *be* in Christ. He chose us to be for the praise of His glory. If God were only interested in our actions, the verse might have said that He chose us to work, serve, witness, or behave for the praise of His glory. Instead, God is clearly interested in something deeper than our activities; He appeals to our identity, that we might *be* for His glory. God sets forth this principle: Our identity in Christ *produces* activities that glorify Him.

Now, let's consider some more real life scenarios. Same instructions as yesterday. Before you start, pray that God would give you insight into these difficult situations.

5 You have just been chosen for a leadership position in your club. Your peers or you may think it's because of the way you look or your superior leadership skills.

• **How might a non-Christian handle a leadership position?**

_____

_____

_____

Now read 2 Corinthians 5:20, Romans 13:1, and Ephesians 2:10.

Being *in Christ* gives you this confidence: Even though you have been chosen by people for earthly purposes, you were placed there by God for eternal purposes.

Now rewrite this as a personal statement:

I may have been chosen for a leadership position, but in Christ

_____

_____

As a Christian, you can handle a leadership position by representing Christ as an ambassador to the people you lead. You do the good works God has prepared for you so that the people you lead see the image of Christ in you.

6 You have made some really dumb choices during high school. You feel the heavy weight of guilt and condemnation, and find it impossible to forgive yourself. Whenever you feel like trying to grow spiritually, you remember what you've done and feel ashamed all over again.

Being in Christ means living for Christ.

If God declares you forgiven, you have no right to condemn yourself.

• **How might a non-Christian handle guilt?**

_____

_____

_____

Now read Colossians 2:13-14 and Ephesians 2:4-8.

Being in Christ gives you this confidence: Even though you feel guilty and condemned by the Enemy, you are completely forgiven and made spiritually alive by God.

Rewrite this as a personal statement:

_____

_____

As a Christian, you can handle guilt by acknowledging the forgiveness you have _in Christ_. If God declares you forgiven, you have no right to condemn yourself. Rather than focusing on your sin, focus on the forgiveness that comes to you in Christ.

7 You have just started a new job, and your co-workers consistently grumble and complain about your boss and work regulations. If it's not the long hours and the bad salary, it's that so-and-so unfairly got the promotion before anyone else. Your co-workers invited you to join in the negative conversation.

• **How might a non-Christian handle this work situation?**

_____

_____

_____

Now read 1 Thessalonians 5:16-18 and Ephesians 4:29.

Being _in Christ_ gives you this confidence: Even though your peers may be negative and complaining, you are to be joyful, prayerful, and thankful in all circumstances.

Rewrite this as a personal statement:

_____

_____

As a Christian, you can handle the temptation to be negative by speaking only things that will benefit those who listen. Rather than joining in the negative conversation, look for ways to encourage others and to defend those who are not around to speak for themselves.

8 You have new roommates. You are already hacked at them because they eat your food, run up the phone bill, and leave a trail of dirty dishes from the living room to the kitchen. To top that off, one of them constantly borrows your clothes without asking, and you have just discovered that one of your favorite shirts is ruined. In your anger, you want revenge.

• How might a non-Christian handle this difficult relationship?

_____

_____

_____

Now read Ephesians 4:25-27, 31-32.

Being in Christ gives you this confidence: Even though you are rightfully angry and want to get even, you have the responsibility to forgive, just as in Christ, God forgave you.

Rewrite this as a personal statement:

_____

_____

As a Christian, you have the gift of God's forgiveness; you don't deserve it any more than your roommate deserves forgiveness from you. In Christ, you have received forgiveness and are called to offer that same forgiveness to others. Find ways to bless those who wrong you.

Be kind and compassionate to one another, forgiving each other, just as, in Christ, God forgave you.

DAY 5 SUMMARY

Finding your identity in Christ teaches you how to handle guilt, leadership roles, negative conversations, and difficult relationship issues.

WEEK ONE SUMMARY

In order to keep from abusing the freedom you will experience upon graduating from high school, you need to embrace the biblical view of your identity. According to God's design, your identity affects your activities, not the other way around; *who you are determines what you do.*

You have been known by your actions up to this point and will probably continue to be known by them. But hopefully it will be because your actions reflect your identity, not determine it. Your biblical identity is in Christ. Who you are never changes because Jesus doesn't change. If you are *in Christ*, you have immediate and permanent security. Finding your identity *in Christ* is the key to your spiritual success and survival during this important transition time of your life.

Make this your prayer today:

Dear Lord, when I leave home, I don't want to give up spiritually. I want to grow during this transition time in my life. Teach me daily what it means to be in Christ. I pray that my actions and reactions to life's situations will reflect this identity. I want to become spiritually mature, not just for when I leave home, but for today. Based on what I've studied this week, I want to grow in these ways:

_____

_____

_____

_____

_____

_____

WEEK 2

Where There's a Word There's a Will

Week 2:

WHERE THERE'S A WORD, THERE'S A WILL

As a naval captain sailed the night ocean, he noticed the light of another ship heading on a crash course with his vessel. The captain, using Morse code, flashed the following message, "This is the *USS Altamaha*. Change your course two miles to the west." After a minute passed, the captain received this flashing message: "You change your course two miles west." Frustrated, the captain sent another warning: "This is the captain of the *USS Altamaha*. Alter your course two miles west." Again the message returned, "You change your course two miles west." Now enraged, the captain warned, "This is the aircraft carrier *USS Altamaha*. You must change your course two miles west!" This time the reply read, "This is the lighthouse. You must change your course two miles west!"

This week you will study God's will. Many Christian students are blown off course spiritually after they leave home because they don't understand God's will. Some students, like the foolish captain, set their own course in life and expect God to give in to their demands.

In this study, you will find that God's Word stands as an immovable lighthouse for your future. The Bible clearly illuminates at least seven points about God's will that can help you chart a safe course. At the end of the week, you should be able to confidently answer the question, "According to God's Word, am I in God's will?" May He shine a beacon of hope into the darkness of your future!

Day 1 False Models
Day 2 To Know Him
Day 3 To Grow in Him
Day 4 To Glow in Him
Day 5 To Flow in Him

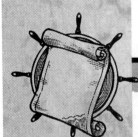

MEMORY VERSE FOR THE WEEK:

Jeremiah 29:11-13

"For I know the plans I have for you," declares the Lord, "plans to prosper you and not to harm you, plans to give you hope and a future. Then you will call upon me and come and pray to me, and I will listen you. You will seek me and find me when you seek me with all your heart."

What comes to mind when you hear the phrase "God's will?"

DAY 1: FALSE MODELS

From the outset of the week, let's review the goal of this study, which is for you to move through this transition in life growing in faith rather than walking away from it.

Over the next few years you will make some of the biggest decisions of your life—whether or not to go to college and if so, where, what to study, where to work, whom to marry. Somehow, you are supposed to find and obey this big mysterious thing called the will of God. This week, you will explore what it means to be in God's will according to His Word.

Unfortunately, there are many misconceptions about God's will. See if your idea of God's will fits into one of these categories:

LINEAR MODEL:
"There's only one way for me to live my life. It's a line between point A and point B. If I get off track, I'm out of God's will for good."

Maybe you think of God's will as a straight line between point A and point B, a course that you must follow or else be lost forever. Sure, this idea has some merit, but it does bring up some problems.

For instance, what if you make a "wrong turn"? What if you go to the wrong college or pick the wrong job? Worse yet, what if you were supposed to meet your spouse at college A in biology class, and your spouse, in rebellion, chose college B? Are you doomed to second best (or worse) because of something that was his or her fault? This is a very scary perspective to live by. It requires that you stay on track every single day, so as not to derail your future and miss anything He might have for you.

So, why is the Linear Model a misconception of God's will?

This is a false model because God can use even our rebellion to bring about His will.

Read Romans 8:28-29. According to these verses, God's will is more a journey than a destination. All along the road in life, God conforms us to the image of His son. Our successes and failures are part of this process. God's will is not confined to a particular church or spouse for you; He cares more about who you are than where you are.

As an example, consider the journey of Philip in Acts 8:26-40. He had a great ministry in Samaria, but God's Spirit led him to Gaza. Along the road, Philip ministered to a eunuch, leading him to saving faith in Christ. In verse 40, you see that Philip actually ended up in Azotus. Interestingly, he never made it to Gaza. So, you can say that God's will for Philip was accomplished on the journey, rather than the destination. If Philip believed the Linear Model, he would have stayed on course to Gaza, possibly missing God's will for him altogether.

Sometimes God's will is found along the road to where you think you are going.

*God cares
more about
who you are
than where
you are.*

COSMIC HIDE AND SEEK MODEL:

"God is way out there in the heavenlies, and I have to find Him and then try to convince Him that I need to know His will."

Maybe your idea of God's will is something like the game "hide and seek." God hides and you seek His will. Again, the idea has some merit because God desires for us to seek Him, but it is not a true picture of God as He reveals Himself in Scripture. Read Matthew 7:9-11 and write down why the Cosmic Hide and Seek Model is not accurate.

_____

_____

If God is a Father who loves to give good gifts to His children, it wouldn't be in His character to consciously and maliciously tease you. He wants to reveal Himself to you. Throughout Scripture, God reveals His desire to guide you. Read each of the following Scripture passages, matching them to what each says about how God wants to relate to you.

____ **Jeremiah 29:13-14**   A. God will instruct, teach, and counsel.

____ **Jeremiah 33:3**   B. God will be found by you.

____ **Psalm 32:8**   C. God will confide in you.

____ **Psalm 25:14**   D. God will tell you things you do not know.

Hopefully you can see from these verses that God does not hide from you. He desires to reveal Himself in ways that you can understand. When it comes to your future, God will not play games.

*God does not
play games
with your
future.*

AFRICA MODEL:

"If I really give myself over to God, He'll send me straight to someplace horrible to be a missionary."

True, God may call you to a foreign country to share Him with other people. But submitting your will to God's hand does not automatically mean you'll be miserable. If you pay attention to what missionaries have to say, you'll find them to be joyful in the midst of what may seem to you like miserable circumstances. They are joyful because they live with the confidence that God who called them there will sustain them. In fact, they will tell you that this calling made them excited. Read again the memory verse for the week. What kind of plan does it say God has for you?

_____

_____

He has plans to prosper you...not to harm you. That's exciting! The God of the universe *wants* you to prosper. The Biblical word picture for "prosper" is of trees blooming in springtime. After a long winter of barren limbs and cold days, springtime offers an exciting, new season of growth. The same is true regarding God's plan for your future. Though you may not always enjoy the process of growth, God will fill you with pleasure and delight along the way. So, if you do end up far from home, you can be confident that you will be filled with great excitement and joy to be there.

GRANDFATHER GOD MODEL:

"God meets my needs. I pray and ask for stuff. He gives it to me. That's all there is to it."

What do most grandparents like to do with their grandchildren? Spoil them. Shower them with gifts. But more than that, they want to shower them with love, affection, and attention. Grandparents enjoy having relationships with their grandchildren more than just giving gifts on Christmas or birthdays.

It's true with God, too. Certainly, He wants to give you good gifts, but more than that, He wants to give you Himself. He wants you to spend time with Him, getting to know Him, learning all about His character and the way He feels about you. He would much rather you seek His *face* than His *hand*. He wants you to put your arms around His neck, not just put your hands in His pockets.

Hebrews 11:6 says, "And without faith it is impossible to please God, because anyone who comes to him must believe that he exists and that he rewards those who earnestly seek him." To some, the greatest reward is for God to reveal His plan. How much more wonderful is it that God would reveal Himself? To seek God solely for the purpose of knowing His plan for your life is short-sighted and self-centered, and you miss out on the greatest reward He can give. . . to know Him intimately.

Do any of these models sound a little too familiar? Fortunately, God's will is much more than a clear linear path, a child's game, a trip across the earth, or Grandpa passing out toys. During the next few days, you will examine Scripture and see that God's will is not really that hard to find. His Word is very clear about His will for your life.

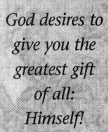

God desires to give you the greatest gift of all: Himself!

DAY 1 SUMMARY

- God desires to reveal Himself to you.
- God's will is more about your journey than your destination.
- Seeking God's heart is more important than seeking His hand.

Make this your prayer today:

Dear Lord,

I confess that my understanding of you doesn't match up with who you really are. I confess that many times, I want to choose my own way rather than try to know your will. Father help me to recognize that you want to reveal yourself and your will to me. Lord, I admit that I struggle the most with the false model of. . .

(Finish your prayer here.)

_____

_____

_____

_____

DAY 2: TO KNOW HIM

Hopefully by now, you are confident that God's will does not have to be a "treasure hunt." During the rest of this week, you will see that God's will is simply His plan for His people, His design for how Christians should live in the world. Through the Bible, God has already revealed this plan in so many ways. The treasure of knowing God's will is yours already! All you have to do is open the pages of Scripture and read the maps by which God shows you the way. Though it may not speak to your specific circumstances, the Bible contains many landmarks that will guide you in the journey ahead. Today you'll discover that step one of God's plan is for you to become intimate with Him. Knowing God is your ultimate destination. It's on the journey to know Him that God reveals His specific plan for your life.

Take a moment as you get started to pray that the Spirit of God would reveal Himself to you as you read His Word. Pray that He would clarify for you today what His will is as revealed in the pages of Scripture.

Read the following Scripture passage, considering what you can know for sure about God's will.

1 Timothy 2:3-4
This is good, and pleases God our Savior, who wants all men to be saved and to come to a knowledge of the truth.

According to the second part of this verse, what does God want?

_____

This brings us to the first and most important point you can know about God's will:

To know God is life's ultimate destination.

1 **It is God's will for you to have a personal relationship with Him.**

Read Matthew 18:12-14. In these verses, you can clearly see that the Father in heaven is not willing for anyone to perish.

Have you ever thought of yourself as a sheep?

On several occasions God compares people with these animals. You may recall Isaiah 53:6 which says, "We all, like sheep, have gone astray, each of us has turned to his own way." 1 Peter 2:25 says that you used to go astray, but now you have returned to the Shepherd and Overseer of your soul. Sheep get lost, and so do people. Sheep need a shepherd for leadership and safety. When they are not wandering off, sheep tend to follow the crowd. This can lead to even more trouble. Think of a time when following the crowd led you into trouble. Describe that time in the box below:

Even spiritual leaders go astray at times. The only reliable shepherd to follow is Jesus. He risked everything to save you. He knows what you need. Only He will guide you in a way that is everlasting and eternal (John 10:27-28). And most importantly, He will never lead you astray. The word "shepherd" in Scripture literally means to guide, to guard, and to protect. That is what Jesus desires to do for you.

So, what is your responsibility in this relationship?

Read this passage, John 10 and circle the words that indicate what sheep do. Put a box around words that indicate what they don't do.

I tell you the truth, the man who does not enter the sheep pen by the gate, but climbs in by some other way, is a thief and a robber. The man who enters by the gate is the shepherd of his sheep. The watchman opens the gate for him, and the sheep listen to his voice. He calls his own sheep by name and leads them out. When he has brought out all his own, he goes on ahead of them, and his sheep follow him because they know his voice. But they will never follow a stranger; in fact, they will run away from him because they do not recognize a stranger's voice.

The best thing a sheep can do is follow the shepherd. He is the one who cares for them and keeps them safe. When sheep hear the shepherd's voice, they follow it because they trust him. That is how you are to follow God. When He speaks, you do what He says because you know His desire is to care for you in every way. You are to build that same intimate, trusting relationship with God that sheep have with their shepherd. Far too many Christians don't trust God in this way. Some are afraid that if they let go of future hopes and dreams, God will lead them to places they don't want to go. How crazy!

You follow God's voice because you trust Him as a shepherd.

Read more of John 10.

I am the good shepherd. The good shepherd lays down his life for the sheep. The hired hand is not the shepherd who owns the sheep. So when he sees the wolf coming, he abandons the sheep and runs away. Then the wolf attacks the flock and scatters it. The man runs away because he is a hired hand and cares nothing for the sheep.

God is not merely looking out for you as if you belonged to someone else. Twice in these verses, He is called the good shepherd. He cares so much for you that He laid down His life to save a sheep like you.

But here is the best part: Your relationship with God means more to Him than what exists between a rancher and livestock. He deeply desires intimacy with you. As you read this next section of John 10, look for the comparison Jesus makes regarding your relationship with Him.

I am the good shepherd; I know my sheep and my sheep know me — just as the Father knows me and I know the Father — and I lay down my life for the sheep.

The relationship between sheep and man can only go so far. But Jesus wants much more than that. In verse 15, He says, "Just as the Father knows me and I know the Father." Jesus compares our intimacy with Him to His intimacy with the Father. Wow! Even while He was on earth, the Son knew the Father perfectly and completely. That's how Jesus wants you to know Him.

All through Scripture, God expresses His will to share intimate fellowship with you. Look up the verses below and match them to the statements that depict God's heart for intimacy with you.

___ Exodus 33:11   A. they might know you

___ Psalm 27:8   B. the surpassing value of knowing Christ

___ Jeremiah 9:23-24   C. face to face, as a man speaks to a friend

___ John 17:3   D. draw near to God

___ Philippians 3:8   E. that he understands and knows me

___ James 4:8   F. your face will I seek

You may have prayed many times to know God's will. God is more interested in you knowing Him. The pursuit of an intimate relationship with Him is far more fulfilling than anything He will lead you to do in life. Before you finish today, state your desire to know God as a sheep knows a shepherd and as a child knows his Father.

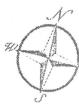

DAY 2 SUMMARY

The most important thing you can know about God's will is that He wants you to know Him intimately.

Make this your prayer today:

Dear Lord,

Oh God, forgive me for being more concerned about knowing your will than knowing you. I believe that you can be trusted as my shepherd. Wherever I need to go in life, you will lead me. Lord, I want to know you in these ways:

_____

_____

_____

_____

_____

DAY 3 TO GROW IN HIM

From yesterday, you know for sure that God desires a personal relationship with you. If you are out of God's will in this regard, the rest of the study will not make sense. The Bible is clear about some parts of God's will. It is so clear that in some cases, you don't have to ask, "What does God want me to do?" Today, you will explore several more Scripture passages that describe some very specific things you can know about God's will for your life.

Read the following passages, considering what each has to say about God's will. Answer the questions that follow.

1 Thessalonians 4:3-8
It is God's will that you should be sanctified: that you should avoid sexual immorality; that each of you should learn to control his own body in a way that is holy and honorable, not in passionate lust like the heathen, who do not know God; and that in this matter no one should wrong his brother or take advantage of him. The Lord will punish men for all such sins, as we have already told you and warned you. For God did not call us to be impure, but to live a holy life. Therefore, he who rejects this instruction does not reject man but God, who gives you his Holy Spirit.

Romans 8:29
For those God foreknew He also predestined [predetermined] to be conformed to the likeness of His Son.

2 Corinthians 3:18
And we, who with unveiled faces all reflect the Lord's glory, are being transformed into His likeness with ever-increasing glory, which comes from the Lord, who is the Spirit.

What do these passages tell you about God's will for your life?

_____

_____

God wants you to grow in Him, to be sanctified. Sanctification might seem like a foreign theological word. Here's an illustration that might clarify its meaning. Consider a Polaroid camera. When you shoot the photo, the picture slides right out. But can you see the picture? Not right away; you have to wait for a little while. Even though you can't see the actual photo at first, it becomes clear with time that the picture was there all along. The image of the picture is on the film. As the image develops, it becomes clearer and clearer.

When Jesus became Lord of your life, God imprinted the perfect image of Jesus Christ on you. You spend the rest of your life letting Him develop that image into the picture others see when they look at your life. What is invisible becomes visible. That's the process of sanctification—letting God work on the outside of you what He already worked inside you at the point of salvation.

This brings us to the second point that you can know for sure about God's will.

2 **To be in God's will, you must be growing daily to outwardly reflect what is inwardly true—that Jesus is in you.**

You may be thinking, "O'kay. It's God's will for me to be sanctified, but how is that going to happen?" If He wanted to, God could wave a magic wand and, poof, you would be like Christ. But if you ask older adults the question, "What has God used to cause growth in your life?" most would answer with the same word; trials. God uses the tough times to produce Christlike character in you.

This is a very important concept for you to understand. Many Christians live with the false belief that God's will is for them to be happy. But the Bible doesn't say that. While God blesses us with many happy moments, His Word says that He wants us to be holy, as Jesus is holy. When you are

Sanctification is the process that allows others to see on the outside of you what God has accomplished on the inside of you.

going through a difficult time, do you gripe and complain, looking for any way to end the trial? Maybe you've even said, "Surely this struggle is not in God's will for me!" Be careful! If you understand that God desires to develop in you the image of Christ, you now have a new perspective on suffering. Write out Romans 5:2-5 in the blanks below:

_____

_____

_____

_____

_____

To have hope you must have _____.

To have character you must develop _____.

To develop perseverance you must go through _____.

Now that you see the purpose for difficult trials, let's look at another aspect of God's will revealed in His Word.

God's will is for you to have the character of Christ; His character is one of joy, prayer, and thanksgiving. Write out 1 Thessalonians 5:16-18 in the blanks below.

_____

_____

Now circle the three things God wants you to do, regardless of your circumstances in life.

As you can see, God's will is for you to give thanks *in* all circumstances. Notice that the verse does not say, "Give thanks *for* all circumstances." This is an important distinction. It would be superficial and dishonoring to God and to those around you to say, "God, thanks for letting my parents get divorced." That's ascribing to God something that He didn't want. Instead, you could say something like, "God, I don't really understand why this is happening, but I thank you for being in control and for being my Father. Thank you for giving me stability and for strengthening me during hard times." Do you see the difference? One perspective dishonors God; the other glorifies Him.

God's will involves even your attitudes.

During hard times, you can be encouraged by James 1:2-4, which says, *"Consider it pure joy, my brothers, whenever you face trials of many kinds, because you know that the testing of your faith develops perseverance. Perseverance must finish its work so that you may be mature and complete, not lacking anything."*

To you, it may sound crazy to consider it "pure joy" to go through a trial. No one enjoys suffering or looks forward to hard times. But the end of verse four gives a beautiful reason to be glad. The finished work of trials is that you would become "mature and complete, not lacking anything." In other words, God uses your difficult trials to mold you into the image of Christ. You may not be able to rejoice over the trial, but you can surely give thanks for what it produces in you.

So, here is the third point to know about God's will:

 It is God's will for you to rejoice, pray without ceasing, and give thanks in all things.

Write about a time in your own life when God used a trial to produce character in you.

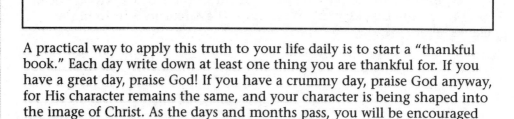

A practical way to apply this truth to your life daily is to start a "thankful book." Each day write down at least one thing you are thankful for. If you have a great day, praise God! If you have a crummy day, praise God anyway, for His character remains the same, and your character is being shaped into the image of Christ. As the days and months pass, you will be encouraged as you read back through your book about all the things God has provided for you.

DAY 3 SUMMARY

* God's will is for you to be sanctified, to grow in Christlikeness and lead a pure and holy life.

* God's will is for you to be joyful, thankful, and prayerful in all circumstances.

Make this your prayer today:

Dear Lord,

Thank you for giving me the stamp of Jesus Christ on the cross. I confess that I do not always live a life that looks pure and sanctified. I also confess that I am not

---

God uses trials to mold you into His image.

always thankful when things go wrong—or right—in my life. These are the things I am thankful for today:

_____

_____

_____

I want to grow in these ways:

_____

_____

_____

DAY 4 TO GLOW IN HIM

So far this week, you have learned that the most important thing you can know about God's will is that He seeks an intimate relationship with you. You have also learned that He desires that you continually grow in Him and be joyful in all circumstances. Today and tomorrow, you will explore several other things Scripture says you can know *for sure* about God's will for your life. The first of these concerns *authority*.

List in Part One of the table below all the authority figures in your life.

PART ONE	PART TWO

Now read the following Scripture passages that speak about authority and answer the questions below them.

Romans 13:1-2
Everyone must submit himself to the governing authorities, for there is no authority except that which God has established. The authorities that exist have been established by God. Consequently, he who rebels against the authority is rebelling against what God has instituted, and those who do so will bring judgment on themselves.

Where does authority come from?

_____

_____

1 Peter 2:13-17
Submit yourselves for the Lord's sake to every authority instituted among men: whether to the king, as the supreme authority, or to governors, who are sent by him to punish those who do wrong and to commend those who do right. For it is God's will that by doing good you should silence the ignorant talk of foolish men. Live as free men, but do not use your freedom as a cover-up for evil; live as servants of God. Show proper respect to everyone: Love the brotherhood of believers, fear God, honor the king.

How does God say you should act toward government authorities?

_____

_____

Christians who don't obey the law make a mockery of the character of God. God instituted the system of authority. Rebellion on your part makes Him look bad. Your obedience, however, brings Him glory.

What does it mean practically to submit to the authorities God has placed in your life? Well, it means you should obey the law; you should obey posted speed limits and stop signs. You should pay your taxes, and you should complete the homework your teachers assign. Basically, if it's the law, you are responsible to obey.

Now read **Ephesians 6:1**. This verse talks about another kind of authority God has placed in your life.

Children obey your parents in the Lord, for this is right. "Honor your father and mother"—which is the first commandment with a promise—"that it may go well with you and that you may enjoy long life on the earth."

Your obedience gives glory to God.

How should you treat your parents? _____

Does Scripture make any exceptions? ❑ yes ❑ no

Though you will examine this verse in more depth during Week Five of this study, it is important for you to acknowledge two things at this point: Your parents are a God-given source of authority, and God did not say that your parents have to be Christians for you to honor them.

Now go back to your list of authorities. Having read what God's Word has to say about them, in Part Two, write down next to each one a practical way you can submit to that authority, and thus be in God's will.

Point four can be summarized in this statement:

4 **For you to live in God's will, you must submit to the authorities in your life.**

Government, parents, teachers, and pastors are established by God for your good (Romans 13:4). The only exception God allows is if submitting to that authority means violating God's Word (see Acts 4:18-20). Otherwise, God's will for you in this area is clearly stated in His Word.

This idea of submission may rub against you. Maybe you feel like this command should only apply to children. . .that adults should have total freedom to do what they want. Truly, to obey earthly authorities honors God. If you struggle with submitting to the law, you will struggle with submitting to God. The world teaches you to rebel and demand individual freedom. As a Christian, you must change your thinking about authority. God's will extends to the way you think about everything in the world.

Read the following Scripture passages and answer the questions that follow.

Romans 12:1-2
Therefore, I urge you, brothers, in view of God's mercy, to offer your bodies as living sacrifices, holy and pleasing to God—this is your spiritual act of worship. Do not conform any longer to the pattern of this world, but be transformed by the renewing of your mind. Then you will be able to test and approve what God's will is—his good, pleasing and perfect will.

What three things are required of you to know God's will?

1. To offer. . . _____

2. Do not. . . _____

3. but be. . . _____

An illustration may help clarify what it means to renew your mind. You may have seen or heard about a new type of alarm clock now on the market. This special device is a combination alarm clock and bedside lamp. What distinguishes this alarm from others is that it wakes you up with light rather than sound. When it is time for the alarm to "go off," the bulb slowly begins to light up. Before long, your entire room is glowing with ever-brightening ultraviolet light. So, as your room is illuminated, you wake up.

The same can be said of your relationship with God. As you seek to know Him through prayer and Bible study, your mind begins to glow with the Truth of God's character. You think about the things of God with ever-increasing intensity. You occupy yourself with the things of God.

Look up Philippians 4:8 and write in the blanks below what kinds of things Christians should think about.

_____	_____
_____	_____
_____	_____

To think about things that are *true* is to think about things that are honest, accurate, and reliable. *Noble* things are dignified, reputable, and worthy of worship. *Right* refers to things that are righteous and conform to a higher authority. To think about *pure* things means that your mind is free of contamination. Things that are *lovely* and *admirable* are pleasing and appealing. *Excellent* refers to something that has outstanding moral goodness and is highly esteemed by others. *Praiseworthy* means something that is commendable; when you commend something or someone, you want it to be recognized for its goodness.

Simply, our minds operate by the "Garbage In — Garbage Out" theory. The Enemy has been putting "trash" in your mind from the day you were born. God wants to "empty" all that trash by the Holy Spirit and fill your mind with His pure, holy Word and full life. This is what it means to conform no longer to the world and to be transformed into the mind of Christ.

5 To be in God's will, wash your mind with the pure water of His Word and thus renew your mind.

DAY 4 SUMMARY

- God's will is for you to submit to the authorities in your life.

- God's will is for you to renew your mind.

Prayer and Bible study illuminate your mind to God's will.

Make this your prayer today:

Dear Lord,

Thank you for clearly revealing to me what your will is for my life. I confess my disobedience to authorities in these ways:

_____

_____

I want to renew my mind. Help me to have the mind of Christ. I know that my thought life needs to reflect Christ in me. I want to improve in these areas:

_____

_____

DAY 5: TO FLOW IN HIM

As you have learned during this week, God's will is not mysterious; He has laid out some very specific guidelines for the way you should live. Most importantly, He wants to know you intimately. Also, He wants you to grow in Him and to be joyful in all situations. He wants you to submit to the authorities in your life and to renew your mind. Today, you will explore two more guidelines laid out in Scripture for how you can be in God's will.

First, review this week's memory verse by writing it in the blanks below:

Jeremiah 29:11-13

_____

_____

_____

_____

_____

_____

Read these Scripture passages and consider what they have to say about God's will for your life. Answer the questions that follow each passage.

2 Corinthians 8:5
And they gave themselves first to the Lord and then to us in keeping with God's will.

What does it mean for you to give yourself first to the Lord?

You belong to God first. Being His child is more important than playing a sport, being a member of a club, dating a particular person, or pursuing a future career. It is even more important than all your religious activities. Praying, worshiping, and serving in the church only have meaning when you give yourself to Him first. Being fully committed to God means that He has control of every area of your life. School, home, friendships, dating relationships, and even Christian activities are all under His direction. This is vital as you seek to understand His will for your life. Many students want to know God's will in regards to their college or career, but have no interest in God's will for other areas in life. Doesn't it seem strange to pray for God's best in a spouse, but then willfully cheat on an exam in school? It's not only strange, it's out of God's will.

This brings us to the sixth thing you can know for sure about God's will:

6 **To be in God's will is to fully surrender every area of life to Him.**

Read the following verses:

1 Kings 8:61
1 Kings 15:14
2 Chronicles 16:9

What is the recurring phrase in these verses?

_____

Without doubt, to be in God's will, you must commit your heart fully to Him. In fact, according to 2 Chronicles 16:9, God is looking for men and women with this depth of commitment. Read this verse again. What does God want to do for people who are fully devoted to Him?

_____

God's will encompasses far more than just your career or your spouse or some other part of your life. He wants to strengthen every area of your life.

One of the worst myths about Christianity is that it is just *part* of your life, another piece of life's puzzle. Maybe you've attempted to find balance in your life, trying to make sure no one area gets out of control. You try to balance your time, your eating, your studying, your rest, your recreation, even your spiritual or religious activities. So, what's the problem with this kind of balance?

Christianity is not just another commitment like all the other commitments in your life. In fact, your steadfast devotion to Christ gives meaning and purpose to the rest of your life. Beyond question, Jesus was the most balanced person ever to live on earth. In His life, you can see a healthy balance that glorified His Father. How was that achieved? Jesus' balance in life came from a radical, sold out, *unbalanced* commitment to the Father. In the same way, if you seek God with a whole heart, a completely *unbalanced* commitment, He will bring order, meaning, and purpose to everything else you do.

Take a moment to evaluate your commitments. Circle the words below that represent areas of your life which have a tendency to command more of your time, affection, and devotion than God.

Academics	Sports	Car
Dating	Friendships	Family
Work	Entertainment	Clubs
Band	Church activities	Drama
	Choir	

Your commitment to God towers over your commitments to everything else in life. Being fully devoted to God brings balance to your life and ensures that you are living in His will.

And now for the last point about God's will. . .

 7 **It is God's will for you to worship Him.**

Read John 4:23-24.

When you think about worship, what comes to mind? Probably you think about worship services on Sunday mornings—singing hymns or maybe a few choruses. You might even think of some time at camp when you really got into the music. The Greek word for worship is "proskyneo," which literally means to bow down.[1] Worship, according to God's word, is more than just a song, it is a posture. One theologian writes,

> *The ancient mode of salutation to one who was considered vastly superior was to fall upon the knees and touch the forehead to the ground, often throwing kisses at the same time toward the superior. In the New Testament, it indicates that presence of a superior to whom one owed reverence and homage, and often accompanied by kneeling or prostrating [lying face down].*

Your devotion to Christ flows into every area of your life.

Worship indicates the posture of your heart.

[1] Hebrew Greek Key Study Bible, NIV, AMG International, Inc., 1996, p. 1669.

God is seeking people who will go beyond singing songs. He desires worshipers who will choose to bow before Him in complete surrender. Going back to the last point, if your heart is fully devoted to God, you will express that commitment in worshiping Him. According to verse 23, in what two ways are you supposed to worship God?

_____ and _____

The spirit refers to the very core of your life. Worshiping God in Spirit means that He is your life; without Him you would be spiritually dead.

Truth is also important in worship. The truth about God goes beyond your good ideas about Him. He will reveal Himself to you through Scripture and by walking with Him. As you discover the truth about God, you have a reason to bow before Him in worship. For example, let's say that you are really confused about your circumstances. God's word says that He is wise and grants wisdom to those who ask (James 1:5). When the truth that God is wise enables you to gain wisdom into your circumstances, your response is to worship Him.

Identify something true about God that gives you a reason to worship Him today.

The Psalms are a great place to learn about worship. The Psalmist expresses his devotion to God throughout the Psalms. As you read them, you will see that his worship flows from what God has done in his life. Read the following Scripture passages, and circle in each *who God is or what He has done.*

Psalm 8:1-3,9
O Lord, our Lord, how majestic is your name in all the earth! You have set your glory above the heavens. From the lips of children and infants you have ordained praise because of your enemies, to silence the foe and the avenger. When I consider our heavens, the work of your fingers, the moon and the stars, which you have set in place. . . how majestic is your name in all the earth!

Psalm 18:1-2
I love you, O Lord, my strength. The Lord is my rock, my fortress and my deliverer; my God is my rock, in whom I take refuge. He is my shield and the horn of my salvation, my stronghold.

Psalm 40:1-3
I waited patiently for the Lord; he turned to me and heard my cry. He lifted me out of the slimy pit, out of the mud and mire; he set my feet on a rock and gave me a firm place to stand. He put a new song in my mouth, a hymn of praise to our God. Many will see and fear and put their trust in the Lord.

Worship doesn't have to be eloquent verse. It can be as simple as "God, I worship you today because you are my Father." Worship is the expression of your heart's affection toward God.

God's will is that you become a true worshiper, one for whom worship is a way of life.

DAY 5 SUMMARY

- God's will is for your to commit your *whole life* to Him.

- God's will is for you to worship Him in Spirit and in Truth.

Before we finish this week's study, let's do a self-evaluation. Go through the list below and put a check by all the ways you can say with confidence that you are in God's will.

God's will is that I. . .

❑ 1. *have an intimate relationship with Him.*
❑ 2. *be sanctified and grow in Him.*
❑ 3. *give thanks in all circumstances.*
❑ 4. *submit to the authorities He has placed in my life.*
❑ 5. *renew my mind.*
❑ 6. *give myself completely to Him.*
❑ 7. *become a true worshiper.*

Make this your prayer today:

Dear Lord,

Thank you for revealing your will to me through Scripture. More importantly, thank you for revealing Yourself. I desire to be in your will according to what your Word says. I want to grow in these areas:

_____

_____

_____

_____

As you see God at work, the natural response is for worship to flow out of your life.

44

WEEK 3

Where There's a Will There's a Way

Week 3:

WHERE THERE'S A WILL, THERE'S A WAY

Military boot camp emphasizes two equally important things: obey the rule book and follow the commander. The military, like any other structured system, operates with rules and guidelines. But the rule book doesn't contain specific instructions for the wide range of scenarios one might encounter on the battlefield. Beyond following the written rules, military personnel must learn to follow the field commander. The commander issues detailed instructions for specific situations. By learning to listen to the officer in charge, enlisted men and women know what to do at any time.

When it comes to knowing God's will, God's Word is the rule book and God is the field commander. As you discovered last week, the Bible lays out some important guidelines that direct your decisions. So what about the specific details of your future? Can God reveal His will in a way that answers your most important questions? Yes! The Bible may only use the words "God's will" a few times, but from Genesis through Revelation, Scripture contains many examples of God's specific leadership by His Spirit. Remember from Day Two of last week, God states His will for you to have an intimate relationship with Him. You looked at the scriptural example of a shepherd and sheep. God doesn't desire this close-knit relationship because He is lonely but because He wants to guide you. Your ability to recognize His voice as a Shepherd *determines* your ability to follow wherever He leads you.

When you face pressure on life's battlefields and the Rule Book doesn't tell you exactly what to do, listen for the voice of your Commander.

Day 1 God Led the Israelites
Day 2 God Still Leads Today
Day 3 Runway Lights
Day 4 Confirmations
Day 5 Your Turn

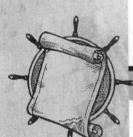

MEMORY VERSE FOR THE WEEK:

Psalm 25:4-5
"Show me your ways, O Lord, teach me your paths; guide me in your truth and teach me, for you are God my Savior, and my hope is in you all day long."

DAY 1: GOD LED THE ISRAELITES

In the same way that God's Word reveals His will, God's Spirit reveals His leadership. Being in God's will according to His Word is a prerequisite for following the leadership of the Holy Spirit. As you discovered last week, part of God's will is for you to develop a listening ear for His voice. You also came to understand that God *wants* to guide you through decisions that affect your life. Therefore, here is a statement you can count on: If you are in God's will according to His Word, you have every reason to expect that He will lead you by His Spirit in life decisions.

In all the discussion about God's will, you may not have heard many people talk about God's leadership. Scripture is full of examples of God's specifically leading his people by His Spirit. Today, you will take a look at several of these in the Old Testament.

First let's review the story of God's leading His people out of their slavery in Egypt into the blessings of the Promised Land. You are probably familiar with the history of the Israelites' journey. Looking closely, you will see the thread of God's leadership spun all the way through the book of Exodus.

When the Israelites became "numerous" (fulfilling God's promise to Abraham), the new king in Egypt became worried and afraid that someday they would rise and fight against him as enemies. So the king "put slave masters over them [the Israelites] to oppress them with forced labor..." (Exodus 2:11). In an effort to reduce the Israelite population, this king ruled that all male children be killed. God, in his divine leadership, saved the life of Moses, who should have been killed along with all the other newborn boys. Moses was even raised by the Pharaoh's daughter!

When Moses was a man, God again provided leadership—this time with a flaming bush. God clearly spoke to Moses about what He wanted him to do.

Read Exodus 3:1-4:17 (Be sure to read this whole selection, for it forms the basis by which you will understand God's leadership!)

What did God tell Moses to do in Chapter three?

_____

How did Moses react to these instructions?

_____

How did God reassure Moses?

_____

Now read Exodus 4:18-5:1 to see what happened.

> *God desires to lead you by His Spirit in life decisions!*

What did Moses do in response to God's leadership?

_____

When Pharaoh refused Moses' request for him to free the enslaved Israelites, God poured hardship upon the Egyptians—plagues of blood, frogs, gnats, flies, livestock, boils, hail, locusts, darkness, and killing of the firstborn. During Egypt's suffering, God protected the Israelites—their livestock was not harmed, the skies did not hail on their land, and the darkness did not envelop their dwellings. This protection confirmed again God's hand of leadership on their lives.

When the Israelites trusted Moses enough to leave Egypt, they began to see God reveal His heart of love for them. God led them every step of the way; He led them into the wilderness, through the wilderness, and eventually into the land of blessing He promised to give them.

Draw a line between the following verses and the phrase that describes what God did for His people.

Exodus 13:21	God led them in order to test their hearts.
Psalm 78:52	God led them for forty years in the desert.
Amos 2:10	God led them like sheep.
Deuteronomy 8:2	God led them by pillars of cloud and fire.

Are you beginning to get the picture? The Israelites, God's chosen people, were enslaved in Egypt, but God literally led them out of captivity. Even when circumstances seemed impossible, God still showed them the way to go. At one point, they came to the Red Sea and the Egyptian army thought they had them trapped. God led them through the sea on dry land (Exodus 14:21-22). When the desert caused them to almost die of thirst, God led them to a well and made the water sweet for them to drink (15:22-27). When Moses died, some people thought God would no longer lead them. But God spoke to Joshua, telling him, "Be strong and courageous, because you will lead these people to inherit the land I swore to their forefathers to give them" (Joshua 1:6).

David would later become the mighty king of Israel. Surely he could lead the people out of his own wisdom and understanding, right? Read the psalm below and circle the words that describe what David wanted God to do.

Psalm 25:1-15
¹_To you, O Lord, I lift up my soul;_ ²_in you I trust, O my God. Do not let me be put to shame, nor let my enemies triumph over me._ ³_No one whose hope is in you will ever be put to shame, but they will be put to shame who are treacherous without excuse._ ⁴_Show me your ways, O Lord, teach me your paths;_ ⁵_guide me in your truth and teach me, for you are God my Savior, and my hope is in you all day long._ ⁶_Remember, O_

God led the Israelites every step of the way.

David cried out for God's leadership.

Lord, your great mercy and love, for they are from of old. ⁷Remember not the sins of my youth and my rebellious ways; according to your love remember me, for you are good, O Lord. ⁸Good and upright is the Lord; therefore he instructs sinners in his ways. ⁹He guides the humble in what is right and teaches them his way. ¹⁰All the ways of the Lord are loving and faithful for those who keep the demands of his covenant. ¹¹For the sake of your name, O Lord, forgive my iniquity, though it is great. ¹²Who then is the man that fears the Lord? He will instruct him in the way chosen for him. ¹³He will spend his days in prosperity, and his descendants will inherit the land. ¹⁴The Lord confides in those who fear him; he makes his covenant known to them. ¹⁵My eyes are ever on the Lord, for only he will release my feet from the snare.

Now go back and look at the number of words you circled that relate God's leadership in David's life. Write those words below.

_____   _____   _____

_____   _____   _____

Hopefully you can see that God wants to be more involved in your life than just telling you what college or career to choose. He wants to lead you just like He led the Israelites and David.

Before we finish today, let's make one more point about God's leadership. Some students live with the attitude that God should lead them because they deserve to know His will. But the psalm above tells us the motive that drives God's leadership. Write verse 8 below.

_____

_____

_____

This verse not only states that God instructs sinners in His ways, it tells you why He does it. The word "therefore" is the key. A good habit when you come across the word "therefore" in your Scripture reading is to ask the question, "What's that 'therefore' there for?" Applied to this verse, the "therefore" shows you that God instructs people in his ways not because the people are good and upright, but because God is good and upright. The basic reason for God's leadership of your sinful life is that He is good. His goodness lights your path and teaches you His ways.

DAY 1 SUMMARY

• God faithfully led His people out of Egypt and through the wilderness.

• By His Spirit, God can lead you, guide you, instruct you, and show you His ways.

God is good; therefore, He leads.

Dear Lord,

Thank you for leading your people through the desert. I believe that you will lead me as well. Thank you for having a plan for my life, and that coming to understand your plan is based on your goodness toward me. (Finish your prayer with the words David used in Psalm 25.)

_____

_____

_____

_____

_____

DAY 2: GOD STILL LEADS TODAY

After the study yesterday, you may have thought, "Great! God provided incredible leadership for the Israelites in the Old Testament. So what about me? Can God lead me like He led them?" Yes! God can and will lead you through the wilderness of your future.

Have you ever wondered why God performed such miraculous signs to lead people back then, but not now? If God wanted to convince you of His plan, He could circle the right college in *The Guidebook to Higher Learning* and write the words, "Go here!" But God no longer needs these tricks to lead His people. Don't waste your time looking for pillars of fire or sweet tasting salt water. God gave them signs and wonders because the Israelites did not possess the Holy Spirit. They needed God to lead them externally because the Holy Spirit didn't exist in them internally.

God has a different, better plan to lead you in these New Testament times. Rather than giving you miraculous signs, He gave you His Holy Spirit. When you accepted Christ, the Spirit God placed in you is part of God Himself. This Holy Spirit in you is as much God as the Father and the Son. In other words, the same God who has a plan for your life lives in your life. You have something the Israelites could never enjoy: God's indwelling Spirit to lead, guide, teach, and direct you in all your ways.

Today you will explore some New Testament passages that can broaden your understanding of how God leads people today. First let's establish that you are a part of God's people.

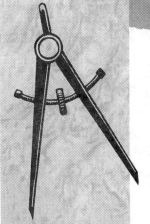

Better than giving you miraculous signs, God gave you Himself!

Read 1 Peter 2:9-10 and check the words below that describe your status according to these two verses:

___ Chosen people   ___ Lost   ___ Hopeless wanderers
___ Spiritual aliens   ___ Royal priesthood   ___ Belonging to the world
___ Holy nation   ___ People of God   ___ Belonging to God

This book was not written to Jewish people living in the holy land. Peter wrote to the Gentiles, non-Jewish people who had no right to claim any status with God. As you can see, God has declared that all who follow Him by faith become a part of His holy nation. You belong to God! You are included in the people of God. This means that God treats you as one of His own. . .a dearly loved child of the Father.

Write 2 Corinthians 1:21-22 in the blanks below:

_____

_____

_____

_____

When a king purchased something, he would put down a deposit which legally secured his claim to that item. This down payment indicated ownership. By placing the Holy Spirit in your heart, God made a deposit on your life, claiming ownership of you now and for all eternity. One thing you can know for certain is that God will take complete care of you, His possession. He will lead you by the Spirit that is in your heart.

Now let's look at some practical examples of God's leadership in the life of Paul.

Read Acts 16:6-10 below. (Don't get bogged down in the names of unfamiliar cities!)

Paul and his companions traveled throughout the region of Phyrygia and Galatia, having been kept by the Holy Spirit from preaching the word in the province of Asia. When they came to the border of Mysia, they tried to enter Bithynia, but the Spirit of Jesus would not allow them to. So they passed by Mysia and went down to Troas. During the night Paul had a vision of a man of Macedonia standing and begging him, "Come over to Macedonia and help us." After Paul had seen the vision, we got ready at once to leave for Macedonia, concluding that God had called us to preach the gospel to them.

How and where did the Spirit lead Paul?

_____   _____

Now read Acts 18:9-11.

One night the Lord spoke to Paul in a vision: "Do not be afraid; keep on speaking, do not be silent. For I am with you, and no one is going to attack and harm you, because I have many people in this city." So Paul stayed for a year and a half, teaching them the word of God.

How did God speak to Paul this time?

_____

You may not have experienced anything like Paul's vision. Certainly Paul was in need of unmistakably clear direction from God. But this word "vision" may not be as strange as you picture it to be. The Greek word "horao" literally means to see, or to perceive with the eye. Sometimes it means to perceive with the mind, or have a feeling of responsibility.[1] Has there been a time when you've said, "I can see myself doing that someday" or maybe, "I just can't see that in my future?"

Write in the box below something you can or can't see in your future.

```
┌─────────────────────────────────────────┐
│                                           │
│                                           │
│                                           │
│                                           │
│                                           │
└─────────────────────────────────────────┘
```

This is the same idea as the word "vision" for Paul. God can help you *see* yourself in His plan for your future. He can reveal which direction not to take in the same manner. The vision may be only a hunch or a slight leaning in one direction over the other. It may be a very clear picture of yourself in a certain career or with a particular person.

Sometimes the Spirit gives much more direct leadership. Write Acts 20:22-23 in the blanks below.

_____

_____

_____

_____

Circle the two words that explain the Spirit's activity in Paul's life.

At times you will feel compelled to do something, go somewhere, or talk to someone. These promptings could very well be the leadership of God's

---

[1] Hebrew Greek Key Study Bible, NIV. AmG Publishers, 1996p. 1656.

Spirit in you. This word for compelled also means "to bind, fasten, or tie as with a chain or cord."[2]

Sometimes the Holy Spirit may cause in you a deep sense of obligation. You might feel, "This is something I must do." In these cases, God's Spirit may be leading you by causing your heart to feel bound, or tied to a certain direction. If God desires you to take a specific path, He will fasten you to it like a cord or chain. Pay attention to these strong positive feelings.

The Spirit led Paul by warning him about hardships and dangers. This feeling of alarm can be as strong as those of duty or obligation. Can you think of a time when you chose not to do something because you had a bad feeling about it? Record that time in the box below:

```



```

The Holy Spirit can warn you against choosing a wrong direction. Your safety may be at stake, or maybe your entire future. If the Spirit lives in your body, it makes perfect sense that He would use your body, including your emotions, to give you leadership.

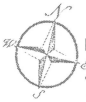

DAY 2 SUMMARY

• God's Spirit lives in you.

• The Holy Spirit reveals His plan through visions, promptings, and warnings.

Dear Lord,

Holy Spirit, thank you for living in my heart. I trust that you know the plans of the Father for my life. I believe that you can and will lead me in the right path. As I listen for your leadership,

I can see in my future. . .

_____

_____

[2] Hebrew Greek Key Study Bible, NIV. AMG Publishers, 1996.

> *God can bind your heart to a particular direction.*

I feel strongly compelled. . .

_____

_____

I feel warned against. . .

_____

_____

DAY 3: RUNWAY LIGHTS

Before you begin today's study, write the memory verse for the week in the blanks below.

Psalm 25:4-5

_____

_____

_____

If you live in accordance with what God has already revealed in His Word about His will, then you can have confidence that He is both willing and able to lead you by His Spirit. To believe this memory verse is to trust that He will show you, teach you, and guide you into the right path. During the next couple of days, you will explore some of the ways God reveals Himself and ultimately, His direction, to His people.

Picture yourself in this situation: You are the pilot of a 747 jet airplane. During the descent toward the airport, the air traffic controller tells you that the entire area is covered by a low-lying fog. She informs you that you will have to land using instruments. Your hands start to sweat, but you remain calm, knowing you've performed this type of landing many times before. Still, nothing will bring you more comfort than to finally see the runway lights stretching out before your eyes. The instruments tell you the story. Eight thousand feet. Six thousand feet. Two thousand feet. You believe the electronic gauges, but your eyes can't see anything out the windshield other than the gray mist of the fog. One thousand feet. You lower the landing gear, still straining to get a glimpse of the runway.

Stop for just a second and answer this question: In this situation, which runway lights would you want to see first through the fog. . .the first two or the last two?

God's Spirit can show you, teach you, and guide you into the right path.

While the last two would let you know where the runway ends, if they are the first lights you see, you may have overflown the landing strip! But if you can see those first two runway lights beaming through the fog, you can rest assured that all the other lights fall into place behind them. You will land safely and avoid a tragic crash.

In a very real way, you are just like that jet pilot. You hold the controls to your future. Many voices may give you advice and encouragement, but ultimately the decisions belong to you. You want to land the "jet" of your life safely on the runway of God's will. You depend on the "instrument" of the Holy Spirit to guide you where you can't clearly see the way. Even though you may feel anxious or even scared, everyone is hoping and praying for your success.

So what are the runway lights God set out to lead you ahead safely? As you've seen in Scripture, God uses many people and many methods to guide His children. He speaks through circumstances, wise counsel, and even your personal desires. But if you try to determine God's leadership based solely on your own desires, you may wreck your life over and over again!

As you peer through the fog of your future, your eyes should strain to see these two bright lights: prayer and Bible study. More than any other method, God will lead your life through the written Word and prayer.

Let's look at these two important guides more closely.

1 THE RUNWAY LIGHT OF SCRIPTURE

Study the following verses about the power of Scripture and answer the questions that follow.

Write Psalm 119:105 below.

_____

Circle the two words describing the role of God's word.

2 Timothy 3:16-17
All Scripture is God-breathed and is useful for teaching, rebuking, correcting and training in righteousness, so that the man of God may be thoroughly equipped for every good work.

How will God equip you for what He has planned for you?

_____

Romans 15:4
For everything that was written in the past was written to teach us, so that through endurance and the encouragement of the Scriptures we might have hope.

Why was Scripture written?

_____

Ephesians 3:4-5
In reading this, then, you will be able to understand my insight into the mystery of Christ, which was not made known to men in other generations as it has now been revealed by the Spirit to God's holy apostles.

What do you understand better by reading Scripture?

_____

2 Peter 1:19-21
And we have the word of the prophets made more certain, and you will do well to pay attention to it, as to a light shining in a dark place, until the day dawns and the morning star rises in your hearts. Above all, you must understand that no prophecy of Scripture came about by the prophet's own interpretation. For prophecy never had its origin in the will of man, but men spoke from God as they were carried along by the Holy Spirit.

What is the word of the prophets compared to?

_____

Where does Scripture have its origin?

_____

God reveals his character through Scripture. Knowing Scripture helps you to know God Himself. Reading Scripture allows you to interact with the living God. As you explored in Week Two, Scripture offers principles about living that help you in your decision-making. God has already revealed some very specific truths to guide you.

God may provide specific guidance through Scripture for particular decisions. Reading the book of Nehemiah, for instance, may inspire a pastor to encourage his congregation to work together on a project and thus bring about revival. Or maybe a student deciding whether or not to go overseas on a mission trip would be encouraged to go by Acts 1:8: "And you will be my witnesses in Jerusalem, and in all Judea and Samaria, and to the ends of the earth."

John White, in *The Fight*, captures this principle of studying Scripture for guidance:

> He [God] wants us to know his mind. He wants us to grasp his
> very heart. We need minds so soaked with the content of Scripture,
> so imbued with biblical outlooks and principles, so sensitive to the
> Holy Spirit's prompting that we will know instinctively the upright
> step to take in any circumstance, small or great...[1]

So, God's Word is the first light that will guide you along your way. Anything that you think God may be leading you to do must be in line with Scripture, or it is not God's plan. The Bible is the only objective standard by which you can base your decisions. **To make a decision that is in conflict with God's Word is never His will!**

2 THE RUNWAY LIGHT OF PRAYER

The second light God uses to reveal His will to you is the beacon of prayer. Prayer is dialogue between God and His people. It is an opportunity for you to talk with Him about your concerns, your joys, your doubts, and your confidences. It is a time when you can be quiet before Him and listen for His voice.

Read **James 1:5-6** and write down God's promise below:

_____

_____

James tells us that God will provide wisdom when we ask Him for it. The psalms are full of prayers for guidance. Read the following Scripture passages and write down what the author is communicating to God.

Psalm 5:1-3, 8

_____

_____

_____

Psalm 63:1-5

_____

_____

_____

The Spirit's leadership will always align with the Bible.

[1] White, John. The Fight. InterVarsity Press, 1976.

Psalm 43:3

_____

Psalm 86:11

_____

Psalm 119:133

_____

David prayed these prayers out of his confidence in the Lord's promise of guidance. He knew God had been faithful to lead in the past and would lead in the future. Notice that David did not always ask for things from God. The verses from Psalm 63 are more of a confession of God's worth than a request for His provisions. As you read in Psalm 5, David lay his requests before God and waited in expectation for God to answer. Finish today's study by laying your requests before God in the prayer below. After you finish writing your prayer, sit quietly and see if the Spirit will bring a clear answer to you. Be sensitive to any inclinations, promptings, or warnings you may sense during prayer.

DAY 3 SUMMARY

Bible study and prayer form the first two runway lights on the landing strip of God's will. With these two visible guides, you can confidently make wise choices.

Dear Lord,

Thank you for allowing me to know you through Scripture and through prayer. I lay these requests before you:

_____

_____

_____

_____

_____

Send forth your light and your truth, let them guide me; let them bring me to your holy mountain, to the place where you dwell.

Psalm 43:3

DAY 4: CONFIRMATIONS

Yesterday you learned that God most often reveals His divine leadership in your life through Bible study and prayer. Using these two runway lights is the safest way to make spiritually sensitive decisions. Thinking about the airport analogy from yesterday, if a pilot sees the first two lights on the airstrip, he can rest assured that all the other lights fall in place behind them.

It's the same way with God's leadership. He wants you to make decisions by faith and with confidence; therefore, He will confirm His leadership in various ways. Sometimes His confirmation comes through circumstances that can be explained by His activity. At times, He will speak to you through the wise counsel of others. Or He may place in your heart a genuine passion for something or someone. These lights of circumstances, wise counsel, and personal desires will further confirm the direction God is leading.

Let's look at them one at a time. This may seem like a lot of work for one day, but hang in there! It will be worth it in the end.

God can confirm His leadership in many ways.

1 THE CONFIRMATION OF CIRCUMSTANCES

Occasionally, circumstances fall so unbelievably in place, there is no doubt that God's hand of leadership is on that particular matter.

Do you remember the unique story of Abraham and Isaac? In Genesis 22, God instructed Abraham to offer his only son, Isaac, on an altar. Read verse 2 below:

Then God said, "Take your son, your only son, Isaac, whom you love, and go to the region of Moriah. Sacrifice him there as a burnt offering on one of the mountains I will tell you about."

Surely Abraham must have been confused by this command. But he trusted the Lord enough to obey. Abraham and Isaac made the journey with the wood for the sacrifice. The story picks up with verses 9-11:

When they reached the place God had told him about, Abraham built an altar there and arranged the wood on it. He bound his son Isaac and laid him on the altar, on top of the wood. Then he reached out his hand and took the knife to slay his son. But the angel of the Lord called out to him from heaven, "Abraham! Abraham!" Here I am, he replied. "Do not lay a hand on the boy. Do not do anything to him."

What an unusual set of circumstances! The Lord, God Himself, told Abraham to sacrifice his son, then an angel of the Lord came along and told him not to go through with it. Who does Abraham believe? He must have hoped the angel represented God's desires, but how would he know for sure? Read verses 13-14 below:

Abraham looked up and there in a thicket he saw a ram caught by its horns. He went over and took the ram and sacrificed it as a burnt offering instead of his son. So Abraham called that place The Lord Will Provide. And to this day it is said, "On the mountain of the Lord it will be provided."

God was leading Abraham to stop the sacrifice of his son. God provided the ram as confirmation of His divine leadership.

Now let's look at a New Testament example.

Read Acts 28:7-10. Use the words below to fill in the blanks in the sentences that follow:

- supplies
- fever
- healed
- all the other sick people on the island
- wife
- everyone else in the chief official's family
- money
- father
- headaches
- dysentery

1. Paul healed a chief official's _____.

2. The man was suffering from

_____ and _____.

3. Paul prayed over him and he was _____.

4. After this _____ came and were healed.

5. When ready to sail, they provided Paul with _____.

You may find it interesting to know that Paul was on the island of Malta because of a shipwreck. He wasn't even supposed to be there! Paul's destination was Rome, but his circumstances allowed him to minister in Malta. As a result of those circumstances, the people of Malta provided the necessary supplies Paul needed to make it to Rome.

Sometimes circumstances can be difficult to interpret. You may come up with several explanations for all the variables in your situation. Maybe you are confused by your circumstances, and don't understand what the Lord is saying through them.

The ram in the thicket confirmed God's leadership.

Henry Blackaby and Claude King offer a few guidelines that may help you interpret God's leadership in circumstances that don't make sense. Read these slowly and carefully.

1. Settle in your own mind that God has forever demonstrated His absolute love for you on the cross. That love will never change.

2. Do not try to understand what God is like from the middle of your circumstances.

3. Go to God and ask Him to help you see His perspective on your situation.

4. Wait on the Holy Spirit. He may take the Word of God and help you understand your circumstances.

5. Adjust your life to God and what you see Him doing in your circumstances.

6. Do all He tells you to do.

7. Experience God working in and through you to accomplish His purposes.[1]

2 THE CONFIRMATION OF WISE COUNSEL

Another avenue God uses to confirm His leadership is through the voices of wise counsel.

Look up and read Ecclesiastes 4:9-12.

According to this passage, why is it good to have wise counsel?

_____

What do you think makes a person wise?

You may be surrounded by wise people. Maybe your parents or some other relatives are wise, or a teacher at school. Possibly, you've benefited from the wisdom of a Sunday School teacher or pastor.

[1] Blackaby, Henry T. and Claude V. King. Experiencing God. The Sunday School Board of the Southern Baptist Convention, 1990.

Why are these people wise? Because they've "been there." They have probably walked through many similar situations in their lives; they are seasoned by life and learning. Take advantage of them. Ask them for advice. Sometimes outsiders have a much clearer view of our lives than we do!

The idea of gaining wisdom through asking for advice is a Biblical principle. Read the following Scripture passages.

Proverbs 13:10b.
...but wisdom is found in those who take advice.

Proverbs 13:20
He who walks with the wise grows wise, but a companion of fools suffers harm.

Proverbs 19:20
Listen to advice and accept instruction, and in the end you will be wise.

Proverbs 23:22-23
Listen to your father, who gave you life, and do not despise your mother when she is old. Buy the truth and do not sell it; get wisdom, discipline, and understanding.

What do all these verses promise?

_____

Consider the relationship between Paul and Timothy. Calling Timothy his "true son in the faith," Paul writes two letters that instruct him about how to live and lead the church. Paul offers Timothy practical advice and instructions, including to remain in Ephesus, to pray for everyone including kings and other authority figures, to train himself to be godly, to set an example for other believers, ...and the list continues. Paul is a mentor for Timothy, encouraging him to "fight the good fight of the faith" (1 Timothy 6:12).

Paul encourages women to have teaching/learning relationships as well.

Read Titus 2:3-4 below.

Likewise, teach the older women to be reverent in the way they live, not to be slanderers or addicted to much wine, but to teach what is good. Then they can train the younger women to love their husbands and children, to be self-controlled and pure, to be busy at home, to be kind, and to be subject to their husbands, so that no one will malign the word of God.

Wise counselors don't tell you what to do; they offer perspective. They share personal objective insights into your life, future, and current decisions. To be a wise counselor, a person must be more than just smart or experienced. Some very intelligent people give very bad advice if they are not interested in the Kingdom of God. If you were to write a job description for a wise counselor, it would certainly include these qualifications:

Wise counselors listen to you, and listen to God.

- Someone who knows you well.
- Someone who loves you in spite of your faults.
- Someone who passionately loves and pursues God.
- Someone who has your best interest at heart.
- Someone who is not afraid to tell you the truth.

Now that you have an idea about what makes someone a good source of wise counsel, think of several people who may fill this role in your life. Write their names in the blanks below:

My wise counselors:

1. _____

2. _____

3. _____

4. _____

③ THE CONFIRMATION OF PERSONAL DESIRES

Perhaps the most enjoyable avenue of God's confirmation is that of your personal desires.

Read Philippians 2:12-13 below.

Therefore, my dear friends, as you have always obeyed—not only in my presence, but much more in my absence—continue to work out your salvation with fear and trembling, for it is God who works in you to will and to act according to his good purpose.

The phrase "to will" in the last part of verse 13 literally means "to wish or desire" and can refer to inclination or love. So according to this verse, God places desires in your heart. As one author describes, God is "providentially forming in you certain desires which will move you in the direction he wants you to go."[2]

Read Hebrews 12:2 below.

Let us fix our eyes on Jesus, the author and perfecter of our faith, who for the joy set before him endured the cross, scorning its shame, and sat down at the right hand of the throne of God.

> *"My desire is to know you lord. My desire is to seek your face. My desire is your holding my heart. My Desire is your desires in me."[3]*

[2] Smith, M. Blaine. Knowing God's Will. InterVarsity Press, 1991.
[3] Lyrics from My Desire by Jamie Smith

Circle the phrase that states the reason Jesus went to the cross.

Jesus went through the agony of the cross *for the joy set before him.* He wanted to go to the cross because He wanted to bring salvation to the world.

Unfortunately, there is a myth that seems to pervade Christianity that says that God doesn't want us to be happy. Maybe you think submitting your will to God's plan for your life means you will be miserable. Actually, it's just the opposite. Submitting your will to God's leadership brings you the ultimate satisfaction. He wants you to be joyful. His desire is for you to be fulfilled (John 10:10).

Write out Psalm 37:3-4 in the blanks below:

_____

_____

_____

_____

What are the requirements for God's giving you the desires of your heart?

_____

_____

Your passion for God will change the desires of your heart.

If you trust in God (giving Him control of your future), and if you find your greatest enjoyment in Him, you can be confident that your desires will be a mirror reflection of His desires for you.

One last thought about God's leadership. (Hang in there; you're doing great!) Many Christians want to know God's complete plan before they take any steps forward. Some will only trust His leadership if they can see the final destination. This is a spiritually dangerous way to live.

Think about driving a car at night. Your headlights don't light the entire trip; they just illuminate 50-75 feet in front of the car. Even if you slow down and stop on the side of the road, you still only see those 50-75 feet. You have to continue moving forward on the road you can see in order to see more of the road ahead of you in the darkness.

It's the same in your relationship with God. If you just stand still in the way that God has revealed, then you won't be able to see what He has planned for you in the future. But if you step out in faith, following the plan that He has illuminated for you, you have every reason to believe that He will light more of the path.

A similar analogy is trying to turn the steering wheel of a parked car. Not only is it hard to turn, but it will usually lock up if you do manage to turn it. The wheel turns much easier when the car is moving. The same is true in seeking God's will. God can guide your life much easier when you are moving in the areas of His will that you do know, rather than focusing on the parts you don't know. Sitting still and attempting to figure out which way to turn before starting to move won't work any better in your spiritual life than it does in the parking lot.

DAY 4 SUMMARY

- God may lead you by circumstances.

- God will speak through other people in your life; listen to wise counsel as you move forward in God's will.

- God has placed desires in your heart.

Make this your prayer today:

Dear Lord,

I want to take steps of faith. Give me just enough confirmation to move in a direction with confidence. Thank you, Lord, for placing in my life these wise counselors. I pray for them now by name.

_____

_____

_____

_____

DAY 5: YOUR TURN

You have been learning all week that God desires to lead you by His Spirit. You know by now that He has a plan for your life, and since He wants you to prosper, He wants to guide you on the journey.

You may be thinking, "That's all great, but how will I know what to do at decision time?" Today, you will meet Angie. She is one of your peers. She, like you, is a senior in high school and will soon be faced with several of the biggest decisions she will ever make. As the end of the year nears, her first decision is what to do after she graduates. Her mind is filled with excitement as well anxiety about her opportunities. What option should she choose? Should she go to college? If so, where? Or should she get a job based on training she already has?

ANGIE'S QUESTIONS:

Today, you will spend some time walking with Angie through her decision process as she asks the question, "Should I go to college?"

Angie knows that before she can expect God's leadership in this specific decision, she needs to make sure she is following God the way He has revealed in Scripture. Daily, she pursues a closer relationship with Him, spending time in prayer and Bible study. She truly desires to be a growing Christian, and God has been faithful to illuminate for her the areas that need work. Her friends have begun to ask her what's different about her.

Though it is not always easy, Angie tries to have a thankful attitude toward God. Through many difficult days in her life so far, she has seen God's faithfulness to produce Christlike character in her. Angie faithfully submits to the authorities God has placed in her life, knowing that God has placed them there for her ultimate good. Being careful to renew her mind, Angie has begun to consider the things she watches on TV, the conversations she has with others, and she is carefully guarding her thought life. As she seeks to grow in her faith, Angie has seen God permeate every area of life. Her heart fully committed to Him, she responds to His goodness with worship.

Of course, Angie is not perfect. God does not expect immediate perfection, though. He expects us to be fully committed to Him. This means we desire to grow in these areas. So, yes, Angie is submitting to God's will as He has laid out in His word. Now, it's decision time.

Angie spends time alone with God, praying and reading Scripture to see where God might be leading her. In praying, she has sensed a growing peace when she thinks about going to college. She feels some anxiety thinking about being alone in a new place, being far from home, getting a roommate, and high academic standards. At the same time, though, she feels waves of God's peace come over her as she prays. It's almost like she senses a divine nod of approval as she pictures herself at college.

She is confident that God will offer her comfort, strength, and guidance in the days to come. In her Bible study, she has come across the following Scripture passages:

Luke 2:52
And Jesus grew in wisdom and stature, and in favor with God and man.

Proverbs 24:3-4
By wisdom a house is built, and through understanding it is established; through knowledge its rooms are filled with rare and beautiful treasures.

Philippians 4:13
I can do everything through him who gives me strength.

#1
Am I in God's will according to His Word?

#2
What do I sense in times of prayer?

#3
What is the Bible saying that might apply?

To Angie, these verses confirmed that God wanted her to grow in knowledge and not to be afraid of being lonely.

Angie sought advice from several people she considers "wise counsel" in her life. First, she talked with her youth minister. Angie knew that he was a godly man and would speak truthfully to her. He encouraged her that going to college seemed the next logical step in her life. Angie had made a significant impact in the youth group, and he knew she would do the same in her college classes, in the dormitory, and in organizations she might join.

Angie and her parents had had somewhat of a strained relationship during the past few years, but she knew they had her best interest at heart. Since Angie was the oldest of three children, she would be the first to leave home—a big adjustment for everyone. Angie knew that money was tight, and her parents told her that sending her to college would significantly strain their financial situation. They were supportive, though, and encouraged her to begin researching costs and expenses for different colleges and that maybe her good grades would qualify her for some scholarships and loans.

Several circumstances put Angie in a good position to apply for college. She had an outstanding academic record and had scored better than most of her peers on the SAT. her high grades and test scores meant she could probably get accepted into the college of her choice. Also, she qualified for some of the top academic scholarships. A couple of Angie's friends were attending a college not far from home, so loneliness seemed not so frightening.

All these avenues seemed to point her toward college. So, Angie asked herself the question, "What do I really want to do?" This one was a little easier, for she had always wanted to go to college. In her heart was a growing desire to help people. She wasn't exactly sure what that meant yet; perhaps she would study medicine or maybe education or some other field. What she did know was that she would need academic training for any of those careers. Since the other sources of God's leadership in her life pointed her toward college, she felt the freedom to act upon her heart's desire and start applying.

YOUR TURN. . .

Hopefully by now you are convinced God has not only revealed His will through His word, but He also desires to lead you by His Spirit as you make practical decisions about your life. You have witnessed the Israelites being led by God out of slavery and into the Promised Land, and you've read about David's confidence in the Lord's leadership of His life. You've seen in Acts evidence of God's leadership in Paul's life. And hopefully, Angie's decision process encourages you that God still leads his people today. Now, it's your turn. . .

For the remainder of today, spend some time walking through a real life decision you are facing right now. Some questions are provided which can serve as a personal worksheet you can use to begin taking steps toward this

#4
What is the perspective of my wise counselors?

#5
Do my circumstances indicate a direction?

#6
In my heart, what do I desire to do?

decision. You may need to stop at certain points along the way to evaluate how you are doing.

Perhaps you are deciding whether or not to go to college. Or maybe you are past that point and are deciding where to go or where to look for a job. Maybe you are deciding about the future of a dating relationship or whether or not to join a certain club at your school. Write down the main question you are asking today in the box below:

What is God's leadership for my life regarding. . .?

[ ]

As you know by now, the first question to face is whether or not you are in God's will according to what He has revealed in His word. Review the statements below and prayerfully consider how you are doing in each of these areas.

❑ I have a personal relationship with God.
❑ I am sanctified and am growing in Him.
❑ I give thanks in all circumstances.
❑ I submit to the authorities God has placed in my life.
❑ I continually renew my mind.
❑ I am committing every area of my life to Him.
❑ I worship God in spirit and in truth.

You don't have to be perfect; what God desires is for you to be growing. You may need to stop right here and deal with some of the areas on the checklist. Then you can confidently move on to the specifics about your future.

Next, what has God revealed to you as you have prayed about this decision? Have you felt "nudged" any particular way? Maybe you answer, "Well, I don't know because I haven't been praying about it." Again, stop here and be praying now. As you remember from Day Three, prayer is one of the most important "runway lights" to knowing God's will for your life.

God has made this clear during my prayer time:

[ ]

And what about Scripture reading? What verses have been meaningful to you as you have been thinking about this decision? Pray now that God would bring to mind Scripture to apply to this specific area of your life.

God has showed me these Scripture verses during Bible study:

Go back to Day Four where you wrote down who you consider to be "wise counsel" in your life. What do these few individuals have to say about this decision? Write their advice in the boxes below:

Wise counselor #1:

Wise counselor #2:

Wise counselor #3:

Now consider your circumstances. What details about your present situation may God be using to confirm His leadership?

These circumstances may be evidence of God's leadership in my life:

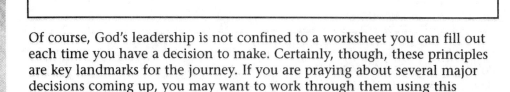

When God's Spirit uses these areas to lead you in a specific direction, you can see how they line up with your own personal desires.

What I really want to do:

Of course, God's leadership is not confined to a worksheet you can fill out each time you have a decision to make. Certainly, though, these principles are key landmarks for the journey. If you are praying about several major decisions coming up, you may want to work through them using this method as a model.

Finish this week by reviewing the memory verse. Write it out in the blanks below.

Psalm 25:4-5

_____

_____

_____

WEEK 3 SUMMARY

- God led His people through the wilderness.

- God leads His people today by the Holy Spirit.

- The Spirit uses visions, promptings, and warnings to move you in a direction.

- Bible study, prayer, wise counsel, circumstances, and your own desires confirm God's leadership.

Make this your prayer today:

Dear Lord,

I admit that I don't know everything about my future. I know that I want my life to glorify you in every way. Lead me in the paths that you desire. Speak to me through your indwelling Spirit and these other ways that confirm your leadership. God, show me what direction to take regarding. . .

_____

_____

_____

_____

_____

WEEK 4

The Dating Game

Week 4:

THE DATING GAME

Everyone needs relationships. Take Pitfall Harry and Harry, Jr., for example. They are the main characters in the Sega game, *Pitfall*. As the story goes, Pitfall Harry has been captured by evil forces in the Mayan jungle. Harry, Jr., for the love of his father, must navigate the dense forest to bring his dad to safety. Along the way, they encounter waterfalls, swing on vines, and even take a ride in a mine car. Harry, Jr. must avoid deadly traps, snares, and vicious crocodiles lurking in the dark marshes. If he can make it to the end, both father and son experience the thrill of victory.

You need relationships, too. Eventually God may bless you with the joy of intimacy that comes in marriage. Before marriage though, comes dating. Dating can be compared to the adventures of Pitfall Harry and Harry, Jr. Along the way you will probably encounter some incredible people and build unforgettable memories. Some of your favorite experiences may happen with the person you are dating. But beware of the pitfalls! Nothing can sidetrack a growing relationship with the Lord more quickly than losing your focus in a dating relationship. Even Christian students often exchange their passionate pursuit of Christ for the pursuit of a companion.

This week you will study the real life adventure called dating. Kept on track, a committed relationship can spur you on toward God and prepare you for tremendous blessings in marriage.

Day 1 The Bigger Picture
Day 2 Pitfalls
Day 3 The New List
Day 4 Non-Negotiables
Day 5 A Dating Covenant

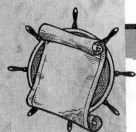

MEMORY PASSAGE FOR THE WEEK:

Ephesians 5:31-32
For this reason a man will leave his father and mother and be united to his wife, and the two will become one flesh. This is a profound mystery—but I am talking about Christ and the church.

DAY 1: THE BIGGER PICTURE

Which of the following best describes how you feel about dating?

❏ "YIKES!"　　　　　❏ Eager　　　　　　❏ Waiting to blossom
❏ A great journey　　❏ Frustrated　　　❏ Emotional roller-coaster
❏ When time permits　❏ Clueless　　　　❏ Other_____

Dating. . .a word that is most feared by some and most enjoyed by others. This word conjures up all kinds of images and feelings for students. Maybe you get scared because of what dating involves—choosing one person above all the rest. Commitment. Pressure. On the other hand, maybe you *live* to date. You can't wait to get a new boyfriend/girlfriend as soon as you've dumped the old one. Or maybe you'd like to date, but no one seems to feel the same about you.

Wherever you fall on the spectrum, one things is true: Dating *after* high school is much different from dating *during* high school.

What about dating are you glad to see change after high school?

What are some of your anxieties about dating after high school?

You can anticipate several key changes in dating after high school:

* After high school, you have much more freedom in your dating life.

    Basically, you get to go **where** you want, go **with** whom you want, do **what** you want, and return **when** you want. Most likely, you won't have a curfew to reckon with, and your nights out are no longer restricted to weekends. You will probably have much less accountability.

* After high school, you have more people to choose from.

    In high school, you know most of the people you date; you know about

Dating is about to take on a whole new look.

their past, their families, their friends, etc. After high school, sometimes you know nothing about the person you go out with. It could be someone you've met at an organizational meeting or someone a friend or coworker has "set you up" with.

- After high school, the stakes are higher.

    Unlike the casual nature of high school dating, relationships in the adult world are often more intense. Couples get "serious" more quickly, and thoughts turn to the potential of marriage. While increased intensity brings deeper fulfillment, it also brings a higher risk of emotional pain and loss if the relationship ends.

What are some of the reasons you date (or would like to!)?

Scripture outlines the destination and the conduct of dating.

The Bible does not specifically address the topic of dating. In biblical days, most young men and women entered marriage relationships pre-arranged by their parents. Now that's a scary thought! It's difficult to admit, but these marriages may have been more stable since adults made the decisions based on the best interests of the couple rather than the couple making the decision based on emotional passion. For this reason, the Bible does not give a pattern for couple relationships before the marriage commitment. Scripture does, however, speak loudly from two angles to the issue of dating: the destination of dating and the conduct of dating.

No doubt, dating can be fun, even if the relationship doesn't lead to marriage. But most people who engage in dating eventually choose someone to marry. Dating is not only an enjoyable end, it's a means by which people choose a spouse. It may sound intimidating for you to think of dating as the pathway to marriage. You have a choice to make. You can choose either to let anxiety keep you in a pattern of shallow relationships that minimize your risk of pain, or you can study the biblical patterns for marriage.

By studying the purpose and meaningfulness of marriage you can gain a new sense of confidence and wider perspective of dating.

You may be wondering at this point, "Why does this study on spiritual growth include this discussion on dating?" To understand the answer you need to see the biblical value of marriage.

Read Ephesians 5:22-33.

What is the passage addressing?

❏ temptations in life
❏ relationships between brother and sister
❏ husband and wife relationships
❏ relationship between God and the Church

This passage has an earthly and a heavenly focus. It addresses both the relationship between husbands and wives, and the relationship between God and the Church. Marriage, as defined by God, should be a living example of Christ's love for the Church.

According to verse 31, what do couples become in marriage?

❏ friends   ❏ one flesh
❏ church members   ❏ all of the above

Marriage forges an inseparable union between husband and wife. In a spiritual sense, the two actually become one. But this "one-ness" is not just for the sake of a happy family. In verse 32, what is the profound mystery that Paul is really trying to explain?

_____

The entire story of the Bible depicts God's passionate love for His people. He desires the most intimate form of union possible. He wants us to be one with Him.

Read these words from Jesus as recorded in John 14:16-20.

And I will ask the Father, and he will give you another Counselor to be with you forever—the Spirit of truth. The world cannot accept him, because it neither sees him nor knows him. But you know him, for he lives with you and will be in you. I will not leave you as orphans; I will come to you. Before long, the world will not see me anymore, but you will see me. Because I live, you also will live. On that day you will realize that I am in my Father, and you are in me, and I am in you.

What does Jesus say you will eventually realize?

_____

God made this intimate one-ness with Him possible through the life, death, and resurrection of Jesus. He wants you to constantly remain aware of the union that exists between you and Him. To do this, God initiated marriage. Marriage is the earthly representation of our relationship to God.

Marriage should exemplify Christ's love.

What happens in a marriage relationship should reflect the kind of love God has for His people. Which words below describe God's love for you?

❏ kind   ❏ giving   ❏ forgiving   ❏ pure
❏ patient   ❏ serving   ❏ sacrificial

God's love for you is expansive. All these words describe facets of His feelings toward you. This is what God wants the world to understand through the picture they see in marriage.

Now, follow this logic:

> If dating leads to marriage,
> And marriage reveals God's love,
> Then, dating should reveal God's love as well.

You not only date today in hopes of finding a spouse, but to complete a visible picture of God-like love. Your conduct in dating should demonstrate kindness, purity, selfless servanthood, protection, and even passionate feelings. Kept in perspective, dating can inspire new levels of devotion in your relationship with God. Then dating, like marriage, becomes a holy illustration through which the world can see Jesus.

DAY 1 SUMMARY

- Dating will change after high school.
- To understand the purpose of dating, you must see the purpose of marriage.
- Dating, like marriage, should reveal God's love for the world.

Dear Lord,

Help me to see dating in the context of your plan for marriage. I pray for every dating relationship I may have to show people your love. Regarding dating I need to. . .

_____

_____

_____

_____

_____

Dating can be a holy illustration.

DAY 2: PITFALLS

Review the memory verse for this week by writing it in the blanks below.

Ephesians 5:31-32

_____

_____

_____

God selected a way to depict His unending covenant of love with humankind. His chosen image is marriage. As you read yesterday, dating, similar to marriage, should visually depict this divine love.

Unfortunately, men and women in dating relationships sometimes lose sight of this holy purpose. Couples go through rough times, and sadly, some relationships end in disaster. Like Pitfall Harry, you need to be able to identify traps that ensnare you, keeping you from enjoying the journey with God. Today you will examine a few of these potentially dangerous pitfalls.

PITFALL #1: MISPLACED IDENTITY

Perhaps you date because you enjoy the social interaction it brings. Or maybe you like having something to do on the weekends. But how do you feel when you sit at home alone on Friday night? If the desire not to be alone drives you to date, you may have the wrong motive. Some people experience anxiety when not involved in a dating relationship. After one relationship ends, another quickly begins. Dating, for some, is more than an activity; it becomes a source of identity. The mind can raise some questions: "If I am dating, I must be attractive. If I'm not dating, how do I know I'm valued by others? If I were special and important, wouldn't people desire my company?"

Your needs for attention, affection, companionship, and worth can motivate you to seek out someone to date. This is a pitfall. While dating may cause you to feel special, it's a horrible source of identity. Boyfriends and girlfriends come and go. Feelings change as quickly as wardrobes. Falling into this identity trap can cause you to lose sight of the only relationship that stands the test of time.

Write Hebrews 13:8 below.

_____

Jesus' love for you never changes because He never changes. Neither will His affection for you, His attention to you, or His presence with you. Dating to find worth stinks. Dating because you have worth in Christ opens the door for you to make others feel valuable. Then dating becomes an avenue through which God communicates His love toward others.

Secure identity is found in Christ.

PITFALL #2: MISPLACED DEVOTION

You may have heard for years about God's passionate love for you. But maybe you struggle with feeling this kind of love toward God. It's much easier to identify feelings you have for a friend or someone you date. In the end, if your feelings for another person eclipse your feelings for God, that other person may become the object of your devotion. Don't feel badly about your emotions. It's normal to have stronger emotions in human relationships than what you experience spiritually.

The real issue, again, is your devotion.

Read Revelation 2:1-6

To whom was this written? _____

What was the problem? _____

_____

> *Your devotion to God should eclipse your devotion to anyone else.*

Do you recall a time in your past when you were most in love with God? Maybe you felt like you were soaring on spiritual heights. The problem with this church in Ephesus goes deeper than feelings. They had forsaken their first love.

The Greek word "aphiemi" is translated "forsaken," the word picture is one of letting go. Your feelings for God will fluctuate, but when you let go of Him, you will fall.

Can you describe a time when you let go of God? What happened?

Read Jeremiah 2:11-13 below.

> *Cistern: a reservoir for storing water.*

". . .Has a nation ever changed its gods? (Yet they are not gods at all.) But my people have exchanged their Glory for worthless idols. Be appalled at this, O heavens, and shudder with great horror," declares the Lord. "My people have committed two sins: They have forsaken me, the spring of living water, and have dug their own cisterns, broken cisterns that cannot hold water."

What two sins does the Lord describe?

_____ and _____

The Israelites constantly struggled to stay connected to God. In this passage God clearly states that to forsake, or to let go of, your devotion to Him is sin.

The second sin is a little more difficult to identify. God says they dug their own cisterns. A cistern is a well that has no underground source; it only catches the rain. In Old Testament times, water from the cisterns was often warm, dirty, and full of bacteria. God grieves that His people have let go of living water. They would rather settle for things in this world that are less than what He has to offer. When you look to dating to bring your life enjoyment and satisfaction, you commit the same sin. Your devotion to God taps a deep well of abundant life which, in turn provides you with something valuable to offer others.

PITFALL #3: MISPLACED FOCUS

If you are like most high school students, you have in mind an ever-expanding "list." This list is a mental image of the perfect person for you. It may include everything from spiritual qualities to body type and hair color.

Describe in the box below your image of the ideal person to marry.

While it may seem harmless—even helpful—to have a list of qualities, it can be dangerous. It's dangerous because chances are high that no one could really match *every single thing* on the list! People inevitably fall short of our extensive expectations. While constructing this list for the "perfect package" may help you steer clear of relational disasters, it may also keep you from dating anyone who doesn't perfectly "measure up" to your mental picture. Remember, you will eventually marry an imperfect person, not a perfect package.

The truth is that God is much more interested in you *being* the right person than you *finding* the right person. As you are learning, God's will is much more about who you are than where you are or even whom you are with. So how do you avoid the pitfall that inevitably results from the list for Penny Perfect or Freddy Flawless? For starters, get rid of the old list and start a new list. For the next two days, you will explore the best lists you can make concerning you and your future mate: lists based on what Scripture says about being a godly man or woman.

You will marry a person not a list!

DAY 2 SUMMARY

- Your identity is in Christ, not in the person you date.
- God should be the object of your heart's devotion.
- You will marry an imperfect person, not a perfect package.

Dear Lord,

Help me know what to do now to avoid these pitfalls in present and future relationships. The trap I most easily fall into is. . .

_____

_____

_____

_____

DAY 3: THE NEW LIST

Knowing what pitfalls to avoid in your dating relationships will help you make the most of the new opportunities you will have at this new stage in your life. The right way, though, to ensure the best in dating is to focus on who you are rather than whom you are looking for. Throughout Scripture, God has revealed some basic principles for the kind of person you should be. When these concepts become part of your character, they permeate through the rest of your life, including your dating relationships.

Today you will construct a different kind of list—one with qualities God calls you to have as a man or woman. Tomorrow you can explore Scripture for a godly "list" of qualities to look for in the person you hope to marry.

The men should stay here to complete today's study. The women can skip ahead a couple of pages for their study. Tomorrow, you will switch.

(NOTE: Only complete the appropriate study for your gender!)

MEN

Today, you will use 1 Timothy 3:2-7 to make a list of the characteristics for yourself. This Scripture will help you understand qualities of the person you are becoming in life in preparation for the person you will marry.

In 1 Timothy, Paul describes the qualities of men who aspire to be deacons, or overseers, in the church. Since God set up deacons as the avenue of leadership for His church, this passage is a model for anyone who desires to be a godly man.

Read the following passage and circle each quality that characterizes a godly man:

Now the overseer must be above reproach, the husband of but one wife, temperate, self-controlled [prudent], respectable, hospitable, able to teach, not given to drunk-enness, not violent but gentle, not quarrelsome, not a lover of money. He must manage his own family well and see that his children obey him with proper respect. . . .He must also have a good reputation with outsiders, so that he will not fall into disgrace and into the devil's trap. Deacons, likewise, are to be men worthy or respect, sincere, not indulging in much wine, and not pursuing dishonest gain. They must keep hold of the deep truths of the faith with a clear conscience.

Let's go through these qualities one at a time. After you read the brief defini-tion, write a practical application to your own life in each box that follows. All your applications will not deal with dating, but they should move you toward godliness.

above reproach: *to be blameless*

A godly man above reproach has no fear of intimacy because he has nothing bad to hide.

```
┌─────────────────────────────────────────────────────────┐
│                                                          │
│                                                          │
│                                                          │
└─────────────────────────────────────────────────────────┘
```

husband of one wife: *faithful*

A godly man who stays devoted to a woman is more likely to stay devoted to God. Faithfulness applies to dating as well as marriage.

```
┌─────────────────────────────────────────────────────────┐
│                                                          │
│                                                          │
│                                                          │
└─────────────────────────────────────────────────────────┘
```

temperate: *from the root word, "temper"*

A godly man controls his temper. Even when angry, he doesn't damage special relationships by exploding in rage.

```
┌─────────────────────────────────────────────────────────┐
│                                                          │
│                                                          │
│                                                          │
└─────────────────────────────────────────────────────────┘
```

self-controlled: *of sound mind*

A godly man controls his thoughts as well as his actions. He guards against lust for women, for money, and for power.

```
┌─────────────────────────────────────────────────────────┐
│                                                          │
│                                                          │
│                                                          │
└─────────────────────────────────────────────────────────┘
```

For this reason a man will leave his father and mother and be united to his wife, and the two will become one flesh. This is a profound mystery—but I am talking about Christ and the Church.

Ephesians 5:31-32

temperate: held within limits

prudent: *one who voluntarily places limits on his own freedom*

A godly man is willing to give up something he enjoys if he knows it would honor someone else.

respectable: *decent, responsible in lifestyle*

A godly man willingly shoulders his responsibilities. He does not neglect or ignore the things he should do.

hospitable: *accepting of others*

A godly man receives others with warmth. He does not allow a "cool image" to keep people at a distance.

able to teach: *skilled to instruct others*

A godly man not only knows what he believes, he also knows how to explain those beliefs to others. He is not ashamed of God's Word or his instructional role.

not addicted to drink: *free from addiction*

A godly man avoids all addictions, including alcohol, drugs, pornography, and the internet.

He who walks with the wise grows wise.

Proverbs 13:20

not violent: *gentle, sensitive to feelings*

A godly man cares about others' feelings. He is sensitive toward those who experience emotional difficulty.

```
┌─────────────────────────────────────────┐
│                                           │
│                                           │
│                                           │
└─────────────────────────────────────────┘
```

not quarrelsome: *not argumentative*

A godly man does not get involved in useless debates or controversies. He seeks to bring peace to hostile relationships.

```
┌─────────────────────────────────────────┐
│                                           │
│                                           │
│                                           │
└─────────────────────────────────────────┘
```

free from the love of money: *not greedy, but generous*

Rather than seeking luxury, a godly man views money as an opportunity to be generous toward others. The issue is not how much money he has, but how he uses it to build God's Kingdom.

```
┌─────────────────────────────────────────┐
│                                           │
│                                           │
│                                           │
└─────────────────────────────────────────┘
```

manage household well: *a manager of time, money, and other resources*

A godly man takes responsibility for his duties as a friend, husband, or father.

```
┌─────────────────────────────────────────┐
│                                           │
│                                           │
│                                           │
└─────────────────────────────────────────┘
```

good reputation: *bearing witness to Christ*

A godly man lives such that others see Christ in him. He avoids appearances of evil so others won't get a bad impression about God.

```
┌─────────────────────────────────────────┐
│                                           │
│                                           │
│                                           │
└─────────────────────────────────────────┘
```

Follow my example, as I follow the example of Christ.

1 Corinthians 11:1

worthy of respect: *worth imitating*

A godly man lives in such a way that if another man imitated him, they both would be acting like Christ.

| |
| |
---

sincere: *true, honest*

A godly man is committed to speaking the truth at all times.

| |
| |

What a list! As you grow into godliness in these ways, you prepare for an incredible marriage. You not only experience deeper intimacy with God, you are becoming the kind of man that godly women find attractive.

To finish this lesson, answer these two questions:

What godly quality from the list do you already see in your life?

| |
| |

What quality from this list needs the most work?

| |
| |

Go to page 89 and write your closing prayer.

WOMEN

Proverbs 31:10-31 offers an in-depth study of the "ideal woman." The writer of Proverbs implies that a man who marries this woman "receives favor from the Lord." Read this passage and underline the actions of a godly woman.

A wife of noble character who can find? She is worth far more than rubies. Her husband has full confidence in her and lacks nothing of value. She brings him good, not harm, all the days of her life. She selects wool and flax and works with eager hands. She is like the merchant ships, bringing her food from afar. She gets up while it is still dark; she provides food for her family and portions for her servant girls. She considers a field and buys it; out of her earnings she plants a vineyard. She sets about her work vigorously; her arms are strong for her tasks.

She sees that her trading is profitable, and her lamp does not go out at night. In her hand she holds the distaff (weaving instrument) and grasps the spindle with her fingers. She opens her arms to the poor and extends her hands to the needy. When it snows, she has no fear for her household; for all of them are clothed in scarlet. She makes coverings for her bed; she is clothed in the fine linen and purple. Her husband is respected at the city gate, where he takes his seat among the elders of the land. She makes linen garments and sells them, and supplies the merchants with sashes. She is clothed with strength and dignity; she can laugh at the days to come. She speaks with wisdom, and faithful instruction is on her tongue. She watches over the affairs of her household and does not eat the bread of idleness. Her children arise and call her blessed; her husband also, and he praises her: "Many women do noble things, but you surpass them all." Charm is deceptive, and beauty is fleeting; but a woman who fears the Lord is to be praised.

Many of these characteristics seem to refer to what this godly woman does. Remember, though, that someone's behavior tells you a lot about his or her identity. Let's go through these activities one at a time. After you read the action and the quality it demonstrates, write a practical application to your own life in each box that follows. All your applications will not deal with dating, but they should move you toward godliness.

full confidence of her husband: trustworthy

A godly woman can be trusted. Unlike those who gossip, godly women know what is appropriate to share, and with whom.

works with eager hands: industrious; hard working

A godly woman is not lazy, expecting others to take care of her. She works hard, whether at school, in an office, or at home.

gets up while still dark: disciplined

A godly woman leads a disciplined life. She studies for school and godliness. She makes the most of her time, not wasting it on pointless activities.

considers a field and buys it: *wise with finances*

A godly woman understands the value of managing money. She knows a good value and refuses to squander money on worldly items.

```


```

arms are strong: *physically fit*

A godly woman stays in good physical shape. She defines physical health, not by unrealistic weights or inches, but by taking care of her body which is God's dwelling place.

```


```

opens her arms to the poor: *compassionate*

A godly woman shows tenderness and compassion to those in need. She keeps from making light of other people's struggles.

```


```

clothed with strength and dignity: *a healthy self-esteem*

A godly woman understands her dignity comes from God. She looks at herself with acceptance and grace because of the grace extended to her by God.

```


```

can laugh at days to come: *sense of humor*

A godly woman, while deep in godliness, sees the lighter side of life. She manages stress and anxiety, knowing that God is in control.

```


```

speaks with wisdom: wise and understanding; speaks the truth

A godly woman possesses spiritual depth. She ponders the ways of God. She offers perspective to others who are confused.

[ ]

fears the Lord: deep love for God

A godly woman passionately pursues God. She knows that in Him she will find her greatest delight.

[ ]

What a list! As you grow into godliness in these ways, you prepare for an incredible marriage. You not only experience deeper intimacy with God, you are becoming the kind of woman that godly men find attractive.

To finish this lesson, answer these two questions:

What godly quality from the list do you already see in your life?

[ ]

What quality from this list needs the most work?

[ ]

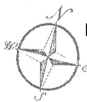

DAY 3 SUMMARY

- The best way to prepare for marriage is to become a man or woman of godliness.

Dear Lord,

Make me the godly person you want me to be. Help me to shift my focus from looking for the right person to being the right person.

_____

_____

_____

_____

Instead, it should be that of your inner self, the unfading beauty of a gentle and quiet spirit, which is of great worth in God's sight.

1 Peter 3:4

DAY 4: NON-NEGOTIABLES

Review this week's passage from memory:

Ephesians 5:31-32

_____

_____

_____

_____

God calls you to become a man or woman who displays His character. Yesterday you read about these qualities of godliness. Rest assured that today His foremost agenda for your life is for you to be conformed to His image.

Before you move on, go back to the final exercise from yesterday where you identified a quality in which you desire to grow. Then pray for God to build this into your life.

Now that you have the right list in mind (the one for yourself), let's look at Scriptural qualities you might look for in a spouse. Like yesterday, you will do this study according to your gender. We'll let the ladies go first today. Men should flip forward to page 94.

(NOTE: Only complete the appropriate study for your gender!)

WOMEN

Read the following passage from 1 Timothy. In it, Paul describes the qualifications for spiritual leadership. While not every man will be a leader in a church, these qualities should be found to some degree in every godly man. After the passage, read the brief description offered for each characteristic. Record any personal insights in each box that follows.

1 Timothy 3:2-7

Now the overseer must be above reproach, the husband of but one wife, temperate, self-controlled [prudent], respectable, hospitable, able to teach, not given to drunkenness, not violent but gentle, not quarrelsome, not a lover of money. He must manage his own family well and see that his children obey him with proper respect. . . .He must also have a good reputation with outsiders, so that he will not fall into disgrace and into the devil's trap. Deacons, likewise, are to be men worthy or respect, sincere, not indulging in much wine, and not pursuing dishonest gain. They must keep hold of the deep truths of the faith with a clear conscience.

above reproach: to be blameless

A godly man above reproach has no fear of intimacy because he has nothing bad to hide.

_____

husband of one wife: faithful

A godly man who stays devoted to a woman is more likely to stay devoted to God. Faithfulness applies to dating as well as marriage.

_____

temperate: from the root word, "temper"

A godly man controls his temper. Even when angry, he doesn't damage special relationships by exploding in rage.

_____

self-controlled: of sound mind

A godly man controls his thoughts as well as his actions. He guards against lust for women, for money, and for power.

_____

prudent: one who voluntarily places limits on his own freedom

A godly man is willing to give up something he enjoys if he knows it would honor someone else.

_____

respectable: *decent, responsible in lifestyle*

A godly man willingly shoulders his responsibilities. He does not neglect or ignore the things he should do.

```


```

hospitable: *accepting of others*

A godly man receives others with warmth. He does not allow a "cool image" to keep people at a distance.

```


```

able to teach: *skilled to instruct others*

A godly man not only knows what he believes, he also knows how to explain those beliefs to others. He is not ashamed of God's Word or his instructional role.

```


```

not addicted to drink: *free from addiction*

A godly man avoids all addictions, including alcohol, drugs, pornography, and the internet.

```


```

not violent: *gentle, sensitive to feelings*

A godly man cares about others' feelings. He is sensitive toward those who experience emotional difficulty.

```


```

not quarrelsome: *not argumentative*

A godly man does not get involved in useless debates or controversies. He seeks to bring peace to hostile relationships.

```
┌─────────────────────────────────────────────────────────┐
│                                                           │
│                                                           │
│                                                           │
└─────────────────────────────────────────────────────────┘
```

free from the love of money: *not greedy, but generous*

Rather than seeking luxury, a godly man views money as an opportunity to be generous toward others. The issue is not how much money he has, but how he uses it to build God's Kingdom.

```
┌─────────────────────────────────────────────────────────┐
│                                                           │
│                                                           │
│                                                           │
└─────────────────────────────────────────────────────────┘
```

manage household well: *a manager of time, money, and other resources*

A godly man takes responsibility for his duties as a friend, husband, or father.

```
┌─────────────────────────────────────────────────────────┐
│                                                           │
│                                                           │
│                                                           │
└─────────────────────────────────────────────────────────┘
```

good reputation: *bearing witness to Christ*

A godly man lives such that others see Christ in him. He avoids appearances of evil so others won't get a bad impression about God.

```
┌─────────────────────────────────────────────────────────┐
│                                                           │
│                                                           │
│                                                           │
└─────────────────────────────────────────────────────────┘
```

worthy of respect: *worth imitating*

A godly man lives in such a way that if another man imitated him, they both would be acting like Christ.

```
┌─────────────────────────────────────────────────────────┐
│                                                           │
│                                                           │
│                                                           │
└─────────────────────────────────────────────────────────┘
```

sincere: *true, honest*

A godly man is committed to speaking the truth at all times.

```
┌─────────────────────────────────────────────────────────┐
│                                                           │
│                                                           │
│                                                           │
└─────────────────────────────────────────────────────────┘
```

MEN

Read the following passage from Proverbs 31. These verses describe the activities of a wife with godly character. While the activities might not apply so much to the world today, the qualities that motivate them are present in godly women. After the passage, read the brief description offered for each characteristic. Record any personal insights in each box that follows.

Proverbs 31:10-31

A wife of noble character who can find? She is worth far more than rubies. Her husband has full confidence in her and lacks nothing of value. She brings him good, not harm, all the days of her life. She selects wool and flax and works with eager hands. She is like the merchant ships, bringing her food from afar. She gets up while it is still dark; she provides food for her family and portions for her servant girls. She considers a field and buys it; out of her earnings she plants a vineyard. She sets about her work vigorously; her arms are strong for her tasks. She sees that her trading is profitable, and her lamp does not go out at night. In her hand she holds the distaff (weaving instrument) and grasps the spindle with her fingers. She opens her arms to the poor and extends her hands to the needy. When it snows, she has no fear for her household; for all of them are clothed in scarlet. She makes coverings for her bed; she is clothed in the fine linen and purple. Her husband is respected at the city gate, where he takes his seat among the elders of the land. She makes linen garments and sells them, and supplies the merchants with sashes. She is clothed with strength and dignity; she can laugh at the days to come. She speaks with wisdom, and faithful instruction is on her tongue. She watches over the affairs of her household and does not eat the bread of idleness. Her children arise and call her blessed; her husband also, and he praises her: "Many women do noble things, but you surpass them all." Charm is deceptive, and beauty is fleeting; but a woman who fears the Lord is to be praised.

full confidence of her husband: *trustworthy*

A godly woman can be trusted. Unlike those who gossip, godly women know what is appropriate to share, and with whom.

works with eager hands: *industrious; hard working*

A godly woman is not lazy, expecting others to take care of her. She works hard, whether at school, in an office, or at home.

gets up while still dark: disciplined

A godly woman leads a disciplined life. She studies for school and godliness. She makes the most of her time, not wasting it on pointless activities.

[text box]

considers a field and buys it: wise with finances

A godly woman understands the value of managing money. She knows a good value and refuses to squander money on worldly items.

[text box]

arms are strong: physically fit

A godly woman stays in good physical shape. She defines physical health, not by unrealistic weights or inches, but by taking care of her body which is God's dwelling place.

[text box]

opens her arms to the poor: compassionate

A godly woman shows tenderness and compassion to those in need. She keeps from making light of other people's struggles.

[text box]

clothed with strength and dignity: a healthy self-esteem

A godly woman understands her dignity comes from God. She looks at herself with acceptance and grace because of the grace extended to her by God.

[text box]

can laugh at days to come: *sense of humor*

A godly woman, while deep in godliness, sees the lighter side of life. She manages stress and anxiety, knowing that God is in control.

```



```

speaks with wisdom: *wise and understanding; speaks the truth*

A godly woman possesses spiritual depth. She ponders the ways of God. She offers perspective to others who are confused.

```



```

fears the Lord: *deep love for God*

A godly woman passionately pursues God. She knows that in Him she will find her greatest delight.

```



```

Remember the "list" you constructed on Day Two? Hopefully what you just read will re-order the qualities you look for in a spouse. Too many Christians place high emphasis on physical beauty or worldly status. These are irrelevant to the One who crafted each person and possesses all wealth.

As you date with marriage in mind, the most helpful exercise you can employ is to narrow the list. Whittle it down to a few non-negotiable attributes that honor God and give Him freedom to bring you to the spouse you need.

One non-negotiable quality should stand out above all others. Anyone you marry should have a growing relationship with God. As you read in Day One, if it is the model for marriage, then it is also the standard for dating.

Read 2 Corinthians 6:14-18.

In this passage, you find the following contrasts:

Righteousness	**vs.**	**Wickedness**
Light	**vs.**	**Darkness**
Christ	**vs.**	**Belial (false gods)**
Believer	**vs.**	**Unbeliever**
Temple of God	**vs.**	**Temple of idols**

The point is clear: These things don't go together. . .not in the church, not in a marriage, and not in dating. God does not say non-Christians are worthless, but that non-Christians have different passions. Unbelievers are not led by the Holy Spirit, so they can't distinguish between personal desires and Spirit-led desires.

This non-negotiable relationship with God does not mean that the person you date should be fully mature. That person, like you, still behaves immaturely at times. What should be evident is a desire to grow. This pursuit of God will eventually lead you both toward maturity in Christ.

Go back to the list you read today about the opposite sex. Pick several qualities that you consider non-negotiable. Write them in the blanks below.

A GODLY LIST

I desire someone who. . .

1. *has a growing relationship with God.*

2. _____

3. _____

4. _____

5. _____

Let this list be your guide in days to come. Set aside your worldly agenda which includes characteristics that don't matter to God. Give God freedom to lead you in this dating process. Who knows? Maybe someday in the future, you will sit down with your spouse, open up this workbook, and show him or her that God blessed you with exactly what you desired.

DAY 4 SUMMARY

- God should determine the list of qualities you look for in a spouse.
- Dating relationships, like marriage, are to be "equally yoked."

Dear Lord,

Guide me as I make decisions about dating. I want this area of my life to honor you. I yield my list of expectations to your sovereign plan.

_____

_____

_____

_____

> *Desire for spiritual growth will lead a person to maturity.*

DAY 5: A DATING COVENANT

Review the memory verse for this week by writing it in the blanks below.

Ephesians 5:31-32

_____

_____

_____

_____

This week you have successfully used God's Word to navigate the confusing jungle of dating. Hopefully you have sharper tools to cut away the world's demands, and a keener eye for avoiding relationship traps.

Before you end this week, you should consider one more hidden danger. This pitfall works like quicksand—the deeper you sink into it, the harder it is to get out.

PITFALL #4:
INTIMACY WITHOUT COMMITMENT.

Commitment paves the way for intimacy.

Let's examine this trap up close.

What are some words or phrases you and your peers use to describe dating? (seeing each other, hanging out, etc.)

```
┌─────────────────────────────────────────────┐
│                                               │
│                                               │
└─────────────────────────────────────────────┘
```

Students masterfully find many ways to rename dating relationships. Couples spend time together, go out, share intimate conversations, get to know each other. Some even kiss, but still refuse to "label" it as dating.

This is more than just a word game; it's a trap! Intimacy is best described as closeness. God designed intimacy in any relationship to happen in the context of a commitment.

Read the following passages and draw a line matching each reference to its corresponding phrase.

1 Samuel 20:16-17   Ruth's commitment to Naomi.

Ruth 1:15-18   God's commitment to Israel.

Genesis 2:24   Jonathan's commitment to David.

Jeremiah 31:33   Husband's commitment to his wife.

The word used to describe commitment in Scripture is "covenant," which refers to a contract or solemn oath. This covenant opened the doorway to intimacy between both parties, whether friendship, marriage, or in relation to God.

Intimacy without commitment leads to insecurity. You don't know what the other person will do with the intimate details of your heart because there is no agreement established.

Do you know anyone who has been hurt by falling into this trap? Describe that person's feeling.

Marriage, as you learned in Day One, is an earthly picture of the covenant relationship between God and humankind. Both contracts allow for openness, vulnerability, and intimate knowledge. To move in the direction of intimacy without the security of a commitment opens your heart to someone who has not agreed to protect it.

Maybe dating commitments cause you anxiety. Possibly you think you will just wait until you are pretty sure you've found the right person to marry before you commit to date. Truly, if dating makes you anxious, the idea of committing to one person for life will terrify you!

Remember, dating is training ground for marriage. You cannot go from being "just friends" straight to husband and wife. If you will not commit in a dating relationship, you are not likely to make the leap of committing to a marriage relationship.

Your willingness to commit now shapes your ability to commit later!

The truth is that your willingness to commit now to dating determines your ability to commit later to a marriage. Marriage is based on solemn vows which describe how spouses will treat each other. You can establish a similar covenant for dating.

Read this covenant below, looking up the verses that correspond with each vow.

A COVENANT FOR DATING

❑ We will treat each other as belonging to God (Romans 14:8).

❑ We will establish accountability to respect the sexual boundaries established by God (Hebrews 13:4, 1 Thessalonians 4:3).

❑ We will encourage one another's growth in the Lord (Hebrews 3:13; 10:25).

❏ We will keep our eyes on Jesus instead of each other (Hebrews 12:1-2).

❏ We will display qualities of godly love (1 Corinthians 13).

If you are in a dating relationship, pray about going through this covenant with that person. Look up the verses together. Discuss adding other vows to the dating covenant.

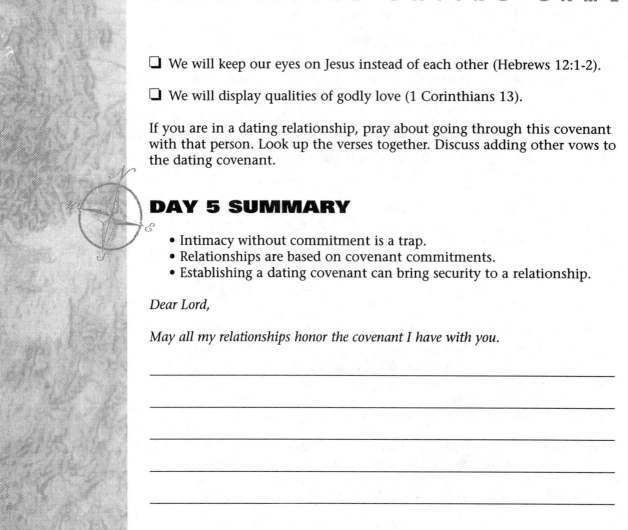

DAY 5 SUMMARY

- Intimacy without commitment is a trap.
- Relationships are based on covenant commitments.
- Establishing a dating covenant can bring security to a relationship.

Dear Lord,

May all my relationships honor the covenant I have with you.

_____

_____

_____

_____

_____

102

WEEK 5

Home Free

Week 5:

HOME FREE

Base camp. The young scout reloaded his backpack and folded up the tent after the two days the troop had been there. He and the rest of the troop had spent two days studying maps, reviewing safety procedures, and getting acclimated to the higher elevation. In the distance he could see the mountain peak. High winds whipped the snow into an icy tornado around the summit. "Are we really going there?" he thought. Base camp was nice, warm, and perfectly comfortable. The troop cook prepared a hot meal while the scout took the last hot shower he would have for five days. "Will it be worth the effort?" he questioned. Whenever he looked toward the peak, something inside him longed for the joyous view from the top. Still, he knew he would miss the comforts of base camp.

Does base camp sound like your home? Comfortable. Safe. But looking out your bedroom window you can see the summit of "Mount Independence." You realize that eventually you'll have to pack up your belongings, say good-bye to family and friends, and begin a new leg of your journey.

This week you will study God's Word as it relates to leaving home. For many Christian students, leaving home means leaving the faith, and they drop out of the spiritual journey for awhile. Others are so eager to get away from home and get on with life that they leave behind all traces of adolescence, including what-ever avenues to spiritual growth they had grown up with.

This is the most critical time for you spiritually. On the road to independence, you will either continue to walk the path of godliness, or you will walk away from it altogether. As you move into the study this week, pray that during the rest of your time at "base camp," God will prepare you to reach the peak of inde-pendence. And when you get to the top, plant a flag for all to see that reads "Glory to God!" Let's move forward. . .

Day 1 Independence Day
Day 2 Loss of Independence
Day 3 The Good Life
Day 4 The Honor Code
Day 5 P.D.H.—Public Display of Honor

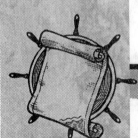

MEMORY VERSE FOR THE WEEK:

Malachi 1:6
"A son honors his father, and a servant his master. If I am a father, where is the honor due me? If I am a master, where is the respect due me?" says the Lord Almighty.

DAY 1: INDEPENDENCE DAY

Consider some ways that you have gained independence in your life so far. Make a list in the box below of these signals of "independence day."

```
┌─────────────────────────────────────────────┐
│                                               │
│                                               │
│                                               │
│                                               │
│                                               │
└─────────────────────────────────────────────┘
```

You may have listed staying at home alone for the first time, getting your driver's license, and dating. The ultimate independence for you probably lies in the next few months—high school graduation.

Relying on these watermarks of independence may be dangerous. Why? In biblical times, boys became men at age 13. The bar mitzvah conferred adult status on boys. At 13, they were free to marry, establish a home, live separately from their parents, and own land. During that time, independence paralleled puberty. When a boy became a man physically, he also became a man socially. Physical maturity meant social independence.

Today, as you know, parental responsibility and authority usually extend through the time you are 18, financially often through college. This pushes the age of independence to 21 or 22, if not later. At the same time, physical maturity is happening sooner. Because of the way society and culture have changed, girls and guys are reaching physical adulthood much sooner than they used to.

Do you see the tension? While physical maturity is happening earlier, social independence is happening later. This tension fuels your desire for independence; you feel ready for it much sooner than society—and your parents—allow you to have it. For many teenagers, gaining social independence means becoming an adult. For them, maturing equals independence.

You are in danger spiritually if your intense desire for independence spills over into your relationship with your heavenly Father. As a Christian, maturity does not equal independence. In fact, it's just the opposite—spiritual maturity means *dependence* on God and on others in the Body of Christ.

Be encouraged. Even though you may ache for independence, there are three ways to avoid this dangerous "spillover."

First, value spiritual freedom. As you learned during the first week of this study, you have freedom in Christ. Before you accepted Christ, according to Romans 6, you were a slave to sin. You lived an impure life, offering your body to what verse 19 calls, "ever-increasing wickedness." Your life was controlled by selfish desires and sinful choices. Read verses 16-18 below.

Don't you know that when you offer yourselves to someone to obey him as slaves, you are slaves to the one whom you obey—whether you are slaves to sin, which leads to death, or to obedience, which leads to righteousness? But thanks be to God that, though you used to be slaves to sin, you wholeheartedly obeyed the form of teaching to which you were entrusted. You have been set free from sin and have become slaves to righteousness.

Now which do you prefer, being a slave to sin which leads to death, or being a slave to obedience which leads to righteousness? Jesus Christ has given you the greatest freedom you could hope for. . .freedom from the death penalty of your sin. Not only that, because the power that raised Christ from the dead lives in you, you are also free from having to sin in the first place. What incredible freedom you have in Christ!

Second, appreciate the other forms of freedom you already possess. A radio talk show host told a story about wanting more in life. She and her family were eating spaghetti when she noticed that she only had three meatballs on her plate. Everyone else had five. She griped and moaned about not having two more meatballs. She accused others of being selfish for not sharing. She complained so much that at the end of the meal, she realized she didn't even enjoy the three meatballs she ate.

Are you like that sometimes? Do you gripe and complain about the things you don't get to do, or the freedoms your parents won't allow? When you do this, you forfeit something of value in view of not having all you want. So maybe you are not completely free of your parents' control just yet. You will be someday. But between now and then, you can value the independence they have given you and enjoy life more along the way.

Third, realize that social independence—freedom from your parents—is only one facet of maturity.

Look up Luke 2:52 and write it in the blanks below.

_____

_____

Now, go back and circle the four ways Jesus grew.

He grew in wisdom (academically) and stature (physically), and in favor with God (spiritually) and man (socially). In the effort to gain freedom socially, you may easily overlook the independence you already enjoy physically, academically, and spiritually.

Longing for what you don't have steals your enjoyment of what you do have.

List the ways you already have freedom of control in these areas:

Academic: _____

_____

_____

Physical: _____

_____

_____

Social: _____

_____

_____

Spiritual: _____

_____

_____

To recap, when you find yourself struggling to gain more freedom than your authority figures are willing to let you have, affirm these things: *I'm free from the penalty of sin and the power of sin. I'm grateful for the freedom that I enjoy already, freedom that goes beyond deciding what I can do socially.* Be careful not to fall into the trap of wanting so much freedom that you forget about the freedom you already enjoy.

DAY 1 SUMMARY

• Spiritual maturity does not equal independence; it equals dependence.

• Social independence is only one facet of maturity.

Make this your prayer today:

Dear Lord,

You know I desire freedom and independence. Help me to understand that depen-

dence on you is the measure of spiritual maturity. These are the ways I want you to help me grow in maturity:

academically: _____

_____

_____

physically: _____

_____

_____

socially: _____

_____

_____

spiritually: _____

_____

_____

DAY 2: LOSING INDEPENDENCE

One person's gain is another person's loss.

In Day One you discovered some ways that your life is already independent of your parents. But, as with most things in life, one person's gain is another person's loss. Take baseball, for instance. When a player steps up to bat and hits a game-winning home run, his team rejoices with the victory. The other team, even though they were winning, now has lost. When it comes to the competition for control of your life, it may seem like you and your parents are on opposite teams. So be aware that at the same time you are gaining independence, they are experiencing a tremendous loss. In the end, your parents want nothing more than to know you are prepared to make mature, adult-like decisions in the real world. When it comes to your independence, they are on your side! Today, you will try to see this transition from your parents' point of view.

How much do you remember about your birth? What about the early days of your life? Your first two years? Anything?

Think back to your earliest childhood memory. Describe it here:

```
┌─────────────────────────────────────────────┐
│                                               │
│                                               │
│                                               │
│                                               │
└─────────────────────────────────────────────┘
```

How old were you? _____

Most people can't remember anything that occurred before they were 3 years old. Even then, they are usually just blurry images without much detail.

Ask your parents about the memory of their first child's birth. Ask them to describe the earliest days of being Mom and Dad. Write down here what one parent describes: (This is part of the study, so if your mom or dad is around, go ask one of them now!)

```
┌─────────────────────────────────────────────┐
│                                               │
│                                               │
│                                               │
│                                               │
└─────────────────────────────────────────────┘
```

Most parents remember being at the hospital, thinking about how much life was about to change. They remember arriving at home with their new baby, midnight feedings, and the endless rank diapers. They recall the new restrictions on their budget. They gave up staying out late with friends and being spontaneous with their free time.

Are your parents mad at you for this? Do they resent you? No! They were happy to give up some of their freedoms in order to take on responsibility for you.

Consider this irony: The freedom they gave up so many years ago to take care of you is the very same freedom you struggle and fight to get. For years, your parents have made countless sacrifices to provide for you; all along, they've known that you would never fully appreciate this effort until the day you are a mother or father yourself, sacrificing your own freedom to raise another generation.

For 17 years, your life, overall, has been your parents' responsibility. Now, they are supposed to just let go. But it's hard to relinquish the responsibilities you value.

Below, write down an area of responsibility that would be difficult for you to give up (varsity sports, club leadership, church group, etc.).

_____

Your parents sacrificed the same freedom you desire.

As you gain independence, your parents lose identity, responsibility, and time with you.

If you think it will be difficult to give up this responsibility, imagine how hard it must be for parents to give up ultimately the most satisfying responsibility—you! Why will this be hard for your parents? Simply, they love you. They want you to make responsible, wise decisions about your life. It's a big step for them to begin trusting these decisions to you.

Besides responsibility, what else will your parents lose when you graduate from high school and leave the house?

Some lose identity. Biblically, identity is tied to parenthood. In the days when the Bible was written, people didn't have last names like we do. They were known by the name of their father. In the original writings, the word "bar" means "son of." When Peter confessed Jesus as the Christ, Jesus declared, "Blessed are you, Simon bar (son of) Jonah, for this was not revealed to you by man, but by my Father in heaven" (Matthew 16:17). Identity was passed from father to child. You can also see this thread of identity linked to parenthood in Proverbs 31, which describes a wife of noble character as one who watches over the affairs of her household, who provides for her family, and whose children rise up to call her blessed.

Even today, many adults find identity in parenthood. They get together with friends and spend much of the time talking about their children. The name "Mom" or "Dad" represents far more than just a set of responsibilities; it is a valued source of identity. In light of this, think about how your parents' identity will change when you leave home. Your parents will lose daily interaction with you. Their activity level may drop considerably. They no longer have you as a reason to be involved with the school system or with the youth group at church. They may miss being around your friends' parents at football games, school events, etc. They will experience the loss of knowing what happens during your day; they know the future may hold only sparse updates. Most importantly, they lose the assurance that you will not make a total mess of your life.

So, what can you do to make this loss easier for them?

• You can demonstrate adult levels of responsibility in your own life.

  Some parents become more strict as Independence Day nears. They fear you are not ready to be responsible for yourself. Show them you can maturely handle adult schedules—getting up in the mornings, doing your own laundry, establishing and maintaining a checking account, taking care of your car, going to church.

  This is a biblical principle. Matthew 25:21 says, "His master replied, 'Well done, good and faithful servant! You have been faithful with a few things; I will put you in charge of many things.'"

• Most importantly, assure your parents that you are ready for adult responsibilities by abiding by their rules while you are at home.

Don't break your curfew, help with the dishes without being told, etc. If you abide by *their* rules, they can be confident you will abide by society's rules (college or workplace) and God's rules when you leave home.

- Another important key to easing this transition for your parents is to acknowledge the difficulty of it for them. Let them cry when you graduate. Be understanding and sensitive when they get upset as you enthusiastically talk about leaving home.

  Say out loud to them, "I know this transition is hard for you, too."

This transition may be harder for your parents than it is for you. Your world will probably be filled with new people and new activities. Their home will lose your presence and all that goes with it. In your family, who do you think is struggling the most with this transition?

_____ me   _____ Mom   _____ Dad   _____ brother/sister   _____ other

So, how can you make this transition easier? Resolve now to live as a responsible adult. Nothing will give your parents greater pleasure than knowing their efforts as parents have produced a mature man or woman who is able to navigate the waters of life — whether calm or rough.

DAY 2 SUMMARY

- The same freedom you long for is the very responsibility your parents give up.

- You can ease this transition for your parents by taking adult responsibilities now, by following your parents' rules, and by acknowledging the difficulty of the transition for them.

Make this your prayer today:

Dear Lord,

Thank you for the freedom you have given me. Help me to begin now to act as a responsible adult. These are the ways I want to begin taking responsibility in my life:

_____

_____

_____

_____

Remember, this transition affects your whole family.

DAY 3: THE GOOD LIFE

Up to this point your parents have been mostly responsible for you. With age and maturity, you have taken on more responsibility for yourself. But living at home perpetuates the "parent makes the rules/child follows them" aspect of the parent-child relationship. When you "leave the nest," you will enjoy much more freedom and control. You can rest assured that during this transition time after high school, your relationships with your parents will change right along with most other aspects of your life.

In a few words, how would you describe the kind of relationship you've had with your mom, dad, step-parent this year?

Look up Ephesians 6:1-3 and Deuteronomy 5:16.

Both of these verses list two benefits of honoring your father and mother. Write these benefits on the lines below:

_____

_____

While only God knows the actual length of your life, you can help determine the quality of it. "That it may go well with you" is an interesting phrase. Think about times when things have *not* gone well for you at home. Describe one or two of those times below:

What do each of those times have in common? For most, you have "the good life" at home when relationships are healthy. Rebellion, conflict, and battles over freedom all produce times that are not so "well." Maybe you've wondered if you will always relate to your parents the way you do now. Whether good or bad, this is another area of your life that is bound to change.

If you have a close relationship with your parents, leaving home can renew your sense of appreciation for all they do for you. You might miss the intimate conversations about day-to-day events. But the change will be good, allowing you to develop independence from them and dependence upon God; hopefully, you will build a Christian life which stands separate from the faith of your parents.

If you have a strained relationship with your parents, leaving home will probably feel like a "jail break" at first. You will enjoy the autonomy and control that come with independence. But the change could be dangerous. Losing touch with your parents may leave you feeling all the more lonely. Making all your own decisions can lead to some damaging mistakes. Unfortunately, too many seniors who "escape" from home become alienated from their parents for many years.

Do you want things in life to "go well with you"? The Bible clearly states the road to take. In the verses below, underline the part which states your responsibility in order to benefit from the promise.

Honor your father and mother, which is the first commandment with a promise— that it may go well with you and that you may enjoy long life on the earth.

You probably do not use the word "honor" every day, but daily you see its presence or absence in relationships. When a husband cancels a business trip to spend time with his family, he honors them. When a mom sacrifices her Saturday in order to take her kids to soccer games, it's an act of honor. When a student speaks highly of a teacher, that's honor.

When you were a child, what did it look like for you to honor your parents?

How has this changed for you as a teenager?

Tomorrow, you will explore more fully the biblical concept of honor and how it applies to real life.

Good life = healthy relationships

Independence from parents means greater dependence on God.

113

DAY 3 SUMMARY

- Your relationships with your parents will change.

- Regardless of the kind of relationships you have with your parents, you are commanded to honor them.

Make this your prayer today:

Dear Lord,

Thank you for my parents. I want things to "go well" with me. Regardless of how long I live, I want to have the "good life." Help me to understand how to honor my parents. . .

_____

_____

_____

_____

_____

DAY 4: THE HONOR CODE

Today, we will look more closely at the concept of "honor." Hopefully, you will be able to answer the following questions at the end of this section:

- What is the scriptural basis for honor?

- How does honor affect the way you relate to your parents?

Webster's dictionary defines honor as "a showing of merited respect." It adds the following synonyms: homage, reverence, deference. The definition continues:

Honor is respect and esteem shown to another. Honor may apply to the recognition of one's right to great respect. Homage adds the implication of accompanying praise. Reverence implies respect mingled with love, devotion, or awe. Deference implies a yielding or submitting to another's judgment or preference out of respect.[1]

[1] Webster's Ninth New Collegiate Dictionary. Merriam-Webster Inc. Publishers, 1984.

According to the definitions above, check the words below which apply to this particular concept of honor:

❏ Respect   ❏ Obligation   ❏ Awe
❏ Title   ❏ Love   ❏ Yielding
❏ Esteem   ❏ Devotion   ❏ Award
❏ Praise   ❏ Submitting   ❏ Dread

If honor is like a house, then these words are like the bricks used to build the house: respect, esteem, praise, love, devotion, awe, yielding, submitting.

Scripture contains many examples of honor. Let's look at a couple of them, starting with the memory verse for this week.

Malachi 1:6
A son honors his father, and a servant his master. If I am a father, where is the honor due me? If I am a master, where is the respect due me?" says the Lord Almighty.

In this passage, God addresses a common problem with his chosen nation of Israel—they do not treat him with honor. There are two key points to recognize in this verse. First, notice that the statement about a son honoring a father parallels the picture of a servant honoring his master. In one sense, to honor is to obey. Submitting to your parents' rules and desires demonstrates respect for them as your authority figures.

You may feel like you don't need an authority figure anymore. Well, don't miss the second lesson of this verse. The verse says, "A son honors his father. . .if I am a father, where is the honor due me?" The honor a son gives his father is an earthly picture of a spiritual truth. As a Christian, God is your heavenly Father. Honoring your earthly father not only pleases your dad, it shows deep respect for God as your foremost Authority figure. Some teenagers live with the attitude that they will honor God, but their dad is not worthy of respect. Be careful! If you never learn to honor an earthly dad whom you can see with your eyes, how could you ever learn to honor a heavenly Father whom you believe in by faith? God gave you a training ground to learn how to honor Him. The student who rebels against his earthly dad will eventually rebel against the authority of his Father in heaven also. Looking at Ephesians 6:1-2, you see that this biblical picture of honor applies as much to your mother as to your father.

Look up Leviticus 19:3 and write it in the blanks below:

_____

_____

Circle the word that describes how you should treat your parents.

Honoring your earthly parents honors your Heavenly Father.

Your version of the Bible might say respect, or fear. Both are words that indicate honor. While this doesn't mean you should live in terror of your parents, it does mean that you should revere them. In other words, the best reason to respect your parents' desires is not out of duty, obligation, or fear of punishment, but out of love for them. Remember from Day Two of this week, your parents demonstrated their devotion to you by caring for you during those years you can't even remember. You can now demonstrate your devotion in return. When you do this, it is a biblical picture of honor.

Look up Daniel 4:34-37. In the blanks below, write the three words from verses 34 and 37 that describe how Nebuchadnezzar honored God for what He had done.

_____ _____ _____

What are some positive things you can say about your parents?

Praise acknowledges a good thing someone has done. When you do well in school, for example, your teacher might praise you with words of encouragement. The word "exalt" literally means "to lift up." This is the same idea contained in the word "glorify." When you exalt or glorify someone, you place him or her in a position higher than yourself.

Nebuchadnezzar showed honor to God by offering him praise and glory. He gave credit to God, the source of his good fortune. Now it may seem too much to ask you to praise your parents, or give them glory. But it wouldn't hurt you to give them proper credit for all they have done for you. One of the best ways to honor your parents is to speak well of them to others. Think about the number of times you hear friends verbally bashing their parents. Clearly, badmouthing your parents dishonors them.

As you get older, you will honor your parents in different ways. For a child, to honor is to obey. After you step out from under your parent's authority, you may disagree with them about plans for your life. At that point, you may not "obey" them fully, but you are still responsible to treat them with proper respect. In the box below, make a list of the ways you hope to honor your parents after you leave their home.

Go back through your list and put a check by the ones that you can start applying today.

DAY 4 SUMMARY

- Biblically, to honor is to praise, exalt, and respect.
- God commands you to honor your parents.
- Honoring your parents teaches you how to honor God.

Make this your prayer today:

Dear Lord,

God, I understand that honoring my parents honors you. Holy Spirit, reveal to me ways that I have treated my parents with disrespect. By your strength and power, I want to show them honor by:

_____

_____

_____

_____

_____

DAY 5:
P.D.H. — PUBLIC DISPLAY OF HONOR

This week's study may have been more difficult for you than some of the previous weeks. You've learned about the struggle for independence and the difficulty many parents have letting go of a child. Maybe you are wondering why this topic is included in a workbook designed to help you grow spiritually after high school. The answer is simple: In an effort to establish independence, many students walk away from anything their parents promoted, even church. In fact, the more your parents forced you to be involved in spiritual growth, the more likely you are to delete church activities when you finish high school and become responsible for your own schedule.

Here is a true statement you can count on: *The greatest way to honor Christian parents is to continue on in faith after you leave home.* It is wonderful for you to show respect, ask for advice, tell them thanks, and spend quality time with them, but nothing will demonstrate honor more than continuing your Christian walk as an independent adult.

If your parents do not have faith in Christ, you still have a responsibility to treat them with honor. If they feel you are "going off the deep end" spiritually, remember what Peter and John said to the religious leaders who told them to stop talking about Jesus Christ. They said, "Judge for yourselves

Maturing means continuing in your faith when you leave home.

whether it is right in God's sight to obey you rather than God. For we cannot help speaking about what we have seen and heard" (Acts 4:19). It is difficult on any occasion to justify disobedience, but if your parents' desires conflict with God's desires, go with God! He is your highest authority on earth, and the One to whom you must answer in heaven.

Your assignment today is to write a letter to your parents. You may use the paper provided here, or your own paper if you want to give it to them when you are finished. The purpose of this letter is to show them honor and to communicate your respect and your appreciation for specific things they have done. If they have set a godly example for you, express your gratitude for showing you what it looks like to follow Christ. If this study has brought to mind ways you have dishonored your parents in the past, offer any words of apology that would be appropriate. Comment on the kind of relationship you want to have with them after you leave home.

The most important thing is to be sincere. Write words that are true, expressing your thankfulness and hope for a good relationship in the future.

When you are finished, pray about an appropriate time to give it to them. If you write it out on separate paper, they will probably keep it forever. You will have given them a priceless treasure. . .the gift of honor.

Make this your prayer today:

Dear Lord,

I don't want to give up on my faith after I leave home. I want to honor you by being the best son/daughter I can for my parents. Show me during the rest of my time at home how to make this transition easier for everyone in my family. As my parents read this letter, I pray they would. . .

_____

_____

_____

_____

_____

Dear_____,

_____
_____
_____
_____
_____
_____
_____
_____
_____
_____
_____
_____
_____
_____
_____
_____
_____
_____

Love,

_____

120

WEEK 6

The Road of
Spiritual Growth

Week 6:

THE ROAD OF SPIRITUAL GROWTH

Two college students decided to take an unusual Thanksgiving break. Instead of going home, to alternate between huge meals and long naps, they decided to take a journey. The only catch was to not even choose a destination. They started out on Wednesday afternoon, excited to see what each day would bring. When they reached major intersections, they would take turns deciding which way to go next.

The two adventurers stopped in town squares, met local folks on crowded street corners, and helped a few stranded drivers on the roadside. Thanksgiving Day they served turkey and dressing to homeless people in a Downtown shelter. On Sunday morning they arrived back in the same place they started. They had gone nowhere, yet they had experienced so much. They both concluded it was the best Thanksgiving they'd ever had. The joy was not in the destination, it was in the journey itself.

Maybe you are a person who likes to know where the road will end. Applied to your faith, if you can't see where God is leading you, you're not sure you want to go. This week you will lay aside your expectations of the outcome of walking with God, and focus on the walk itself.

Spending eternity with God is beyond your wildest imagination. But today God cares more about your enjoyment of the journey. Let's keep moving forward.

> *Day 1 Spiritual Inventory*
> *Day 2 The Finish Line*
> *Day 3 Childlike Maturity*
> *Day 4 The Walk of Maturity*
> *Day 5 Meeting With God*

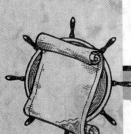

MEMORY VERSE FOR THE WEEK:

Hebrews 5:13-14
"Anyone who lives on milk, being still an infant, is not acquainted with the teaching about righteousness. But solid food is for the mature, who by constant use have trained themselves to distinguish good from evil."

DAY 1: SPIRITUAL INVENTORY

As you set out on this part of the journey, stop and recognize that you have come a long way already. For five weeks you have studied God's Word as it relates to your transition from high school to the great beyond. Pause for a second and say a prayer of thanks to God for strengthening you and revealing Himself to you so far.

Go back to the very first week of the study. Look up the words you used to describe yourself spiritually in the questionnaire on page 3. Rewrite those words or phrases on the lines below.

_____

_____

Just like every other area of your life, things are about to change spiritually for you as well. Even if you stay at home after you graduate, or attend the same church in which you grew up, spiritual growth will take on a whole new look.

Take a few minutes to fill out the following worksheet. Give yourself at least 3-5 minutes to think and write.

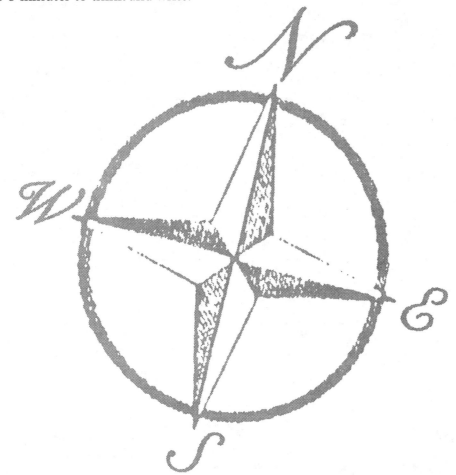

SPIRITUAL GROWTH WORKSHEET

In the blanks provided, record the sources of your spiritual growth over the past four years. Specifically list the names of Sunday School teachers, Christian friends, parents or mentors, camps, mission trips, retreats, and quiet times. Include anything that has helped you grow spiritually in high school.

Hopefully you came up with an extensive list. Isn't it wonderful to see how God has provided for your spiritual development? He has surrounded you with support and nourishment to bring you to this point. Take a moment to thank God for His many spiritual blessings toward you.

Now, the next step may be a little more difficult. Go back through your list and put an X by any source of spiritual growth that will not be available to you when you leave home. You may be able to call a former Sunday School teacher now and then, but if that person will not be a consistent source of spiritual growth in the future, mark an X by his or her name. If you will not be a part of camps and high school retreats after you graduate, mark them off, too.

After marking the Xs, how many sources of growth remain on your list?

_____

For many students, the list is pretty slim. From this activity you may be able to conclude that graduation means major change in the spiritual growth department. The people and events that carried you along and challenged you to walk with God may be left behind when you leave home. Spiritually, it's time to sink or swim. During the first year away from home, most high school Christians drop out of the spiritual race. They don't know how to grow without all these people and events helping them along. But this doesn't have to be your story. In fact, by this time next year you could be spiritually stronger than ever before. The Bible, God's Holy Word, can show you the path to a spiritually bright future.

Look up Hebrews 5:11-14.

What did these people need to be taught?

_____

What word picture is used in verse 12 to describe this teaching?

_____

_____

Write verse 14 in the blanks below.

_____

_____

_____

Circle the word that describes the source of this spiritual training.

Spiritually it's time to sink or swim.

The writer of Hebrews is describing the difference between someone who is a spiritual infant and one who is spiritually mature. Infants need to be trained. Adults train themselves.

Try to visualize these two scenes.

SCENE ONE:

You are having dinner at a friend's house. Your friend has a little sister named Abbey who is almost two years old. Abbey is learning to eat with a spoon, but she still has trouble finding her mouth. Baby food is all over the baby! She has more applesauce on her bib than in her tummy. Abbey gets so much in her hair that she ends up with a mohawk. Of course, she's giggling, and she plays with her meal as if it were a toy.

As an observer, what is your perception of Abbey?

SCENE TWO:

You are having lunch at a nice restaurant. Two executive businessmen sit down at the table next to you. They are both dressed in dark suits, white starched shirts, and impressive ties. One of the executives orders the barbecue ribs. When he gets his order, you notice that he is eating like an animal. Barbecue sauce stretches from ear to ear. He wipes his hands — not on the napkin, but on his nice white shirt. He drizzles more sauce on his tie and begins to laugh out loud. By the end of the meal, he has made a huge mess.

As an observer, what is your perception of this man?

The scenes are similar. Food covers both the infant and the executive, and they both seem to be having a good time. But as an observer, you probably had very different reactions. Most people find the infant cute, or even comical. Babies are supposed to be messy, so it's a sweet, cute picture. Children are accustomed to being fed, so it's okay for them to make a mess when they feed themselves. On the other hand, most people think the executive is gross. The scene is disgusting because adults are supposed to know how to feed themselves.

A hallmark sign of physical maturity is when an infant begins to feed herself. The same is true for you spiritually. You know you are moving toward maturity as a believer when you begin to feed yourself. Relying on youth ministers, Sunday School teachers, and events like camp are fine for the young Christian, but as a high school senior it may be time to learn how to use adult utensils to take in spiritual nourishment on your own.

Fill in these blanks based on Hebrews 5:12-14.

Infants need _____.

Adult need _____.

Children need to be taught _____.

Solid food is for the _____.

Mature Christians train _____ to _____.

Below you will find a list of spiritual activities which are appropriate for either infants or adults. While adults can always benefit from reviewing the basics of Christianity, infants are clearly not ready for adult expressions of faith. Use the words "milk" and "meat" to designate each activity as appropriate for the spiritually young, or mature.

_____ Ask questions about God's existence.

_____ Go through a basic discipleship course.

_____ Teach a children's class.

_____ Learn about witnessing.

_____ Give up Spring Break to go on a college mission trip.

_____ Disciple someone else.

_____ Pray for an hour about the needs of others.

_____ Go with church visitation to witness to others.

_____ Attend church.

_____ Read basic Bible stories.

_____ Minister within the church.

_____ Lead a Scripture discussion.

Finish today's study by evaluating your own spiritual activities. Do they look more like milk or meat? You probably do a combination of both. After today's summary, write out a prayer that states your desire to grow spiritually from infancy to adulthood.

Growing up = feeding yourself

Solid food is for the mature who have trained themselves.

DAY 1 SUMMARY

- Things are about to change for you spiritually.
- Spiritual infants need to be taught.
- Spiritual adults train themselves.

Make this your prayer today:

Dear Lord,

It is time for me to grow up as a Christian. During this next year I want to. . .

_____

_____

_____

_____

_____

DAY 2: THE CALL TO MATURITY

Today you will study the concepts of infancy and maturity more in depth. Before you start, write the memory verse below.

Hebrews 5:13-14

_____

_____

_____

_____

_____

You have looked at Hebrews 5:11-14 already. This time read through Hebrews 6:3.

We have much to say about this, but it is hard to explain because you are slow to learn. In fact, though by this time you ought to be teachers, you need someone to teach you the elementary truths of God's word all over again. You need milk, not solid food! Anyone who lives on milk, being still an infant, is not acquainted with the teaching about righteousness. But solid food is for the mature, who by constant use have trained themselves to distinguish good from evil. Therefore let us leave the elementary teachings about Christ and go on to maturity, not laying again the foundation of repentance from acts that lead to death, and of faith in God, instruction about baptisms, the laying on of hands, the resurrection of the dead, and eternal judgment. And God permitting, we will do so.

Let's define a couple of the words in verse 12 a little more in depth.

"you need someone to *teach* you. . ."

This word for "teach" means that the person being taught is a student, pupil, or disciple. To be a student means more than to gain knowledge. It also means that the will of the pupil is shaped by the teacher. So, as a student of Scripture, your goal should be to gain understanding *and* to shape your life according to what it says.

"the elementary truths of God's Word. . ."

Elementary things are the most basic parts. In this verse "elementary" refers to a point of Christian doctrine. The word "elementary" literally means "starting point." Hebrews 6:1-2 lists five starting points that form the foundation of faith. Write them out below.

Elementary = starting point

1. _____

2. _____

3. _____

4. _____

5. _____

6. _____

1 Spiritual infants know they should repent, but the spiritually mature change their lifestyle.

Repentance is the first step for a newborn Christian. It actually means a 180° turn, or as a drill sergeant would say, "about face."

Read Acts 17:30.

What are some ways you have repented from sin since becoming a Christian?

2 Spiritual infants ask questions about God's existence, but the spiritually mature convince others that He is real.

What could be more basic for a Christian than to have faith in God? Still, many believers have a difficult time believing! Maybe you have hit points along the road where you really doubted God's existence. Don't feel guilty. . . doubting is normal. Learning to have confidence in the One you can't see with your eyes is part of the process toward spiritual maturity.

In what ways have you doubted God?

```


```

3 Spiritual infants can perform religious rituals, but the spiritually mature understand the meaning behind the ritual.

Another basic point of Christian doctrine is "instructions about baptism." Since the days of Jesus' life on earth, baptism has been a symbol of starting over. You may have seen many baptisms as a child before you ever understood what baptism meant.

Are there any church rituals that you do not understand well enough to explain to someone else? baptism, communion, tithing, marriage,. . .

```


```

4 Spiritual infants need ministry, but the spiritually mature engage in ministry.

The next point of basic Christian doctrine deals with the laying on of hands. Look up and read Acts 6:1-6. The twelve apostles lay their hands on seven men. What were these men chosen to do?

_____

Think about your youth group. If it is like many others, it is probably designed to meet the spiritual needs of the average teenager. So, at what point do you think a teenager can help meet someone else's needs?

Write out some things you have done to minister to others.

[ ]

5 and **6**
Spiritual infants are aware of the resurrection of the dead and eternal judgment, but the spiritually mature live in light of these two realities.

Lastly, Hebrews 6:2 lays out two more basic points of Christian doctrine for spiritual infants to understand: the resurrection of the dead and eternal judgment. Believing that a dead man came back to life is difficult. It's illogical and unnatural. Hollywood makes horror films about dead people stepping out of the grave.

Read 1 Corinthians 15:12-14.

If Christ had not risen from the dead, what would that say about your faith?

_____

Now read Hebrews 9:27.

If in fact Jesus did come out of the grave and you know that you will stand before Him in judgment, what implication does this have on your life today?

[ ]

These six points of doctrine may not seem so "basic" to you. According to Hebrews 5 and 6, they are the milk of Christianity. If you have difficulty grasping these concepts, then you are not ready to feed yourself solid food. But don't be discouraged if you are still spiritually young. Like an infant grows into adulthood, you can grow to full maturity as a Christian.

Write out the first half of Hebrews 6:1 below.

_____

_____

Maturity =
finish line

The writer challenges these people to "go on to maturity." This Greek word "telos" literally means "goal." If "elementary" refers to starting point, "maturity" refers to finish line. A mature person has reached the goal, purpose, objective, which is the finish line. He or she is fully grown, measuring up to the standard of being fully devoted and truly obedient to God.

God says the same thing to you today. Now is the time for you to leave the elementary teachings about Christ and press on toward the finish line of spiritual maturity. If you have elementary questions about basic points of Christian doctrine, ask them. Make a list of questions that may seem childish in your eyes to ask, but you are in need of a solid answer. Then sit down with someone who is spiritually mature and have that person show you the answers in God's Word. Afterward you will look back and discover that you have taken a few more steps down the road to maturity.

DAY 2 SUMMARY

- Elementary truths are the starting point.
- Maturity is the finish line.
- Now is the time to move toward maturity.

(Write your own prayer here.)

_____

_____

_____

_____

_____

DAY 3: THE WALK OF MATURITY

In the last two days you may have thought, "Wait a minute. I've been taught all my life that I'm supposed to come to God with the faith of a child. Are you telling me this is wrong?" Today you will see the biblical difference between child-likeness and childishness.

Read Matthew 18:1-6 below:

At that time the disciples came to Jesus and asked, "Who is the greatest in the kingdom of heaven?" He called a little child and had him stand among them. And he said: "I tell you the truth, unless you change and become like little children, you will never enter the kingdom of heaven. Therefore, whoever humbles himself like this child is the greatest in the kingdom of heaven. And whoever welcomes a little child like this in my name welcomes me. But if anyone causes one of these little ones who believe in me to sin, it would be better for him to have a large millstone hung around his neck and to be drowned in the depths of the sea."

What were the disciples asking?

_____

Who did Jesus say is the greatest?

_____

What child-like quality does Jesus encourage?

_____

Jesus said, "unless you change and become like little children,. . . ." Since Jesus said He wanted the disciples to become humble, what problem in their hearts was he probably addressing?

_____

For centuries the church has identified seven deadly sins. The first of these is pride. A proud person claims to be self-sufficient. He boasts about himself. She points to her accomplishments and declares them great. Jesus said that the passport to enter the gates of heaven is stamped with the word "humility." Children have no problem admitting a need. A little boy comes to Mom to tie his shoes. A little girl may sit and cry until Dad fixes the problem. When it comes to being needy, children are humble. Jesus proclaims this as great.

Read Matthew 21:15-16.

In Jesus' time, children were not important. Until a boy or girl reached the age of 12, he or she had no value in society. To some adults children were considered a nuisance. In this story, what were the children doing?

_____

Why do you think this upset the religious leaders?

```
┌─────────────────────────────────────────┐
│                                           │
│                                           │
│                                           │
│                                           │
└─────────────────────────────────────────┘
```

The passport to heaven bears the stamp "humility."

In their own eyes, the chief priests and the teachers of the Law knew all the answers. They had come to the conclusion that Jesus was a false messiah. They ignored His wonderful miracles and grew angry instead. They refused to acknowledge Him as King.

In contrast, the children believed. They saw the wonderful miracles and got excited. They declared Jesus to be wonderful, and praised Him as Lord.

In this story, what child-like quality does Jesus encourage?

_____

Read Luke 10:21-22.

When Jesus refers to "these things," He is speaking about the power of God which is available to His followers. From whom are these truths hidden?

_____

To whom has the Father chosen to reveal these things?

_____

Child-like = humility

Why do you think that God would reveal the mystery of His Kingdom to children rather than to people who were considered wise by the world?

```
                                                          
                                                          
                                                          
                                                          
                                                          
```

Some smart people can be obnoxious with their knowledge. Children don't claim to know much at all. Smart people have answers. Children ask questions. Smart people trust in their education. Children trust in their parents. A child demonstrates tremendous faith in the people who care for him.

What child-like quality does Jesus encourage here?

_____

Now you have a clearer picture of child-likeness. Fill in the blanks below:

Children are not proud, but _____.

Children offer _____ to God.

God reveals Himself to children because of their _____.

In these ways, you too should remain child-like. Child-like humility, praise, and faith can lead you into a more mature experience of Christ.

Now, see what God's Word says about childishness. Read 1 Corinthians 13:11-12.

How did Paul describe himself as a child?

1. I _____ like a child.

2. I _____ like a child.

3. I _____ like a child.

How do children talk, think, and reason?

```
┌─────────────────────────────────────────────────────┐
│                                                       │
│                                                       │
│                                                       │
│                                                       │
│                                                       │
└─────────────────────────────────────────────────────┘
```

When Paul said he thought like a child, he used the word "phroneo." This word not only refers to having a mindset, but it also involves the will and affections. Children think and care about different things from adults. Spiritual children still think and care about the world. Money, possessions, and being in control rank high on the list of priorities. Spiritual adults learn to think differently about who they are and what they do.

Paul uses the word "reason" which means to make sense of something. Non-Christians find ways to make sense of the world. But, without God, a non-Christian is bound to draw childish conclusions. Even spiritually young people often misunderstand God's heart as they try to make sense of their circumstances. Spiritual adults may not always have the answers, but they know that God is in control.

According to 1 Corinthians 13:11, what did Paul do when he became a man?

❑ Got married.
❑ Started ministry.
❑ Put away childish things.
❑ All of the above.

It's alright to act childish if you are a child. But God never intended for you to remain spiritually childish. Childishness is immaturity.

This is what the Lord says: "Let not the wise man boast of his wisdom or the strong man boast of his strength or the rich man boast of his riches, but let him who boasts boast about this: that he understands and knows me, that I am the Lord, who exercises kindness, justice and righteousness on earth, for in these I delight," declares the Lord.

Jeremiah 9:23-24

Match the verses on the left with the corresponding statements on the right.

_____ James 1:2-4

_____ 1 Corinthians 2:6

_____ Ephesians 4:13

_____ Philippians 3:15

_____ Hebrews 6:1

_____ Philippians 3:16

A. The mature understand the message of wisdom.

B. The mature have a certain view of things.

C. The mature attain the whole measure of the fullness of Christ.

D. The mature leave behind elementary teachings.

E. The mature have grown through testing and trials.

F. The mature live up to what they have already attained.

The childish remain immature, but the child-like become mature.

This must be one of the greatest mysteries of God: Those who are childish remain immature, but those who are child-like become mature.

Now that you have studied the difference between childishness and child-likeness, let's put your knowledge to the test. Label each of the following statements with a "+" for mature and a "-" for childish.

_____ My faith is in God alone.

_____ Being a Christian is the same as being good.

_____ God helps me understand my circumstances.

_____ I go to church to help others grow.

_____ I care about sports as much as I care about God.

_____ I think the Bible says something about. . .

_____ I want my life to give God praise.

_____ There may be many ways to get to God.

_____ I love helping people understand God.

_____ Perfect church attendance is an excellent spiritual goal.

_____ My salvation comes from what Jesus did, not me.

Even the most mature Christian you will ever meet *will* be child-like in humility, praise, and faithfulness. What he or she *won't* be is childish.

DAY 3 SUMMARY

- Jesus encourages child-likeness.
- Childishness is immature.
- Maturity is the goal of child-like faith.

Write your own prayer here.

_____

_____

_____

_____

_____

DAY 4: THE WALK OF MATURITY

For three days you have studied the goal of spiritual maturity. You know that to be mature you must move beyond the milk of elementary teachings and begin to "ingest" solid food. You will practice feeding yourself solid spiritual food during Week Seven. Today and tomorrow you will consider some real life examples of spiritually mature individuals that you can use as models for your own growth.

Begin today by writing this week's memory verse, which emphasizes the goal of maturity.

Hebrews 5:13-14

_____

_____

_____

_____

Who is the most spiritually mature person in your life?

_____
| |
| |
_____

What about this person causes you to see him or her as mature in the Lord?

_____
| |
| |
| |
_____

Read Jude 14 and 15. (The book of Jude has only one chapter.)

You may not be familiar with this character, Enoch. What can you learn about his spiritual maturity from these two verses?

Enoch is only mentioned two other times in the Bible, both of which give a wider window into Enoch's faith in God.

Read Hebrews 11:5-6.

Enoch is mentioned here for two reasons. Write them in the blanks below.

Because of his faith, Enoch was _____.

He was commended because _____.

While we don't know much about Enoch, we do know that his life brought God pleasure. According to verse 6, what pleases God?

_____

Now read Genesis 5:21-24.

What phrase occurs twice in reference to Enoch?

_____

Enoch walked with God.

This is the heart and soul of Enoch: he walked with God. By his faith, Enoch brought pleasure to God. This must have been so special to God that He included this phrase twice to honor Enoch in His eternal Word. Walking with God is even more significant when you read what the rest of the people were doing.

Read Genesis 6:5-8.

Which words describe humanity?

❑ Loving   ❑ Evil sometimes
❑ Wicked   ❑ Evil all the time

Which words describe God's heart?

❑ Pained   ❑ Furious
❑ Happy   ❑ Grieved

In the midst of his anguish over the hearts of mankind, one man found favor in the Lord's eyes. Who was it?

_____

Read verse 9.

What three phrases describe his life?

_____

_____

_____

In the rest of Genesis 6, God gives Noah a detailed description of everything he needed to do to build an ark. Undoubtedly, you picture a ship, but Noah had never even seen a boat before! Imagine building a vessel larger than a football field without knowing what the finished product would look like! Write verse 22 to discover Noah's response to God's instructions.

_____

Now do you see why God was so pleased with Noah? Like Enoch, Noah walked with God. By obeying God in faith, both Enoch and Noah brought God tremendous pleasure. Enoch and Noah are beautiful examples of spiritual maturity.

Noah walked with God.

Let's look at a woman in Scripture, Mary, who also models mature faith. Read the following account from Luke 10:38-42.

As Jesus and his disciples were on their way, he came to a village where a woman named Martha opened her home to him. She had a sister called Mary, who sat at the Lord's feet listening to what he said. But Martha was distracted by all the preparations that had to be made. She came to him and asked, "Lord, don't you care that my sister has left me to do the work by myself? Tell her to help me!" "Martha, Martha," the Lord answered, "you are worried and upset about many things, but only one thing is needed. Mary has chosen what is better, and it will not be taken away from her."

What word in verse 40 describes Martha's state of mind?

_____

What do you think she was doing?

_____
| |
| |
| |
| |
|_____|

Martha was obviously bothered that she was doing all the work while Mary did nothing to help. Martha assumed that Jesus would also be upset if He understood the situation. She asks Him to tell Mary to get busy; instead, He rebuked her. And you know it was serious because He said her name twice!

Read verses 41-42 again.

According to Jesus, how many things really matter? _____

Mary was doing something right. She had chosen something better than Martha's frantic preparations. Go back to verse 39 and record what Mary was doing.

_____

In these two women, you can see the difference between spiritual maturity and immaturity. Notice that Martha was not doing anything evil or sinful. In fact, by saying that what Mary was doing was better, Jesus implies that Martha's activities were actually good. The problem with Martha's focus was that she was preparing for a guest who had already arrived. In the end, she traded intimacy for activity. Instead of doing things *for* Jesus, she should have taken time to be *with* Jesus. Gourmet meals and clean homes will all disappear, but intimacy with the Savior lasts forever.

Take a moment as you conclude to calculate the time you spend completing spiritual activities. How much time would you say that you spend during a typical week at church services, fellowships, Bible studies, and/or other religious activities?

_____ hours

How much time during a typical week would you say you spend sitting at the feet of Jesus like Mary?

_____ hours

Mary was spiritually mature. She wasn't trying to shirk her responsibilities. She knew many things had to be done, but she also knew that nothing was more important than being with Jesus. The same is true for the spiritually mature today.

Sometime during this week, talk to that person you identified at the start of today's study as a mature believer. Ask them about their time alone with God. Find out how they feel about spiritual activities when they go for days without praying or reading Scripture. Resolve in your heart to follow this example of faith.

Mary walked with God.

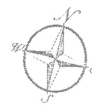

DAY 4 SUMMARY

- Mature Christians walk with God.
- Faith pleases God's heart.
- No activity—spiritual or otherwise—matters more than being alone with Jesus.

Write your own prayer here.

_____

_____

_____

_____

_____

DAY 5: MEETING WITH GOD

Write this week's verse from memory.

Hebrews 5:13-14

_____

_____

_____

As a point of encouragement, if you have made it this far in the workbook, you are doing a *great* job of training yourself. Don't give up during the next two weeks. Your spiritual future may depend on it! Pause now to pray for endurance from God.

All week you've studied about growing up into mature faith. You have looked at milk and meat activities, and the supreme importance of being with Jesus.

By way of review, what biblical woman was engaged in an activity that Jesus encouraged?

_____

What was she doing?

_____

Wait a minute! Since when is sitting considered an activity? How can a person who is not actively working for the Lord be considered mature?

Mary, in fact, was being active, even while she was sitting. What kinds of things do you think she was doing?

```



```

Sitting with Jesus is spiritual activity.

According to this example, spiritual maturity is not measured by how much you do, but by whom you are with. Mary was actively relating with Jesus. She listened to Him, shared with Him, and looked at Him. As well, Mary was engaged in the activity of adoring and loving Jesus. Being alone with Jesus is not a passive waste of time. Rather, one-to-one time with Him brings meaning and purpose to all your other spiritual activities.

Far too many Christians equate maturity with ministry activity. For you to grow up spiritually, you must begin to measure maturity in terms of depth of relationship with God.

What person are you closest to in this world (your most intimate relationship)?

_____

In the box below, write some factors that make this relationship so close.

```



```

If possible, imagine a relationship so intimate that it makes the relationship you just described seem like an acquaintance. That's how deep God wants to go with you!

Maybe you are not very familiar with verses that describe God's passion to meet with you. Let's do a scriptural study on this theme.

Read Genesis 3:8.

What was the Lord doing?

❏ Shouting   ❏ Walking   ❏ Hunting

Rather than join God on His evening stroll through the garden, Adam and Eve hid from Him. Sin severed their intimate fellowship with their Creator.

Read the following verses from Exodus. Underline the recurring phrase.

Exodus 25:22
There, above the cover between the two cherubim that are over the ark of the Testimony, I will meet with you and give you all my commands for the Israelites.

Exodus 29:42-43
For the generations to come this burnt offering is to be made regularly at the entrance to the Tent of Meeting before the Lord. There I will meet you and speak to you; there also I will meet with the Israelites, and the place will be consecrated by my glory.

Exodus 30:6
Put the altar in front of the curtain that is before the ark of the Testimony—before the atonement cover that is over the Testimony—where I will meet with you.

Exodus 30:36
Grind some of it to powder and place it in front of the Testimony in the Tent of Meeting, where I will meet with you.

In case this point escaped you, here it is plainly: God wanted to meet with His people. According to these verses, where was God going to meet with them?

_____

God gave the Israelites specific instructions for building a tabernacle, which literally means "residency" or "dwelling place." Even the name Tent of Meeting magnifies God's desire to relate to His created people. Bible teacher Beth Moore adds some commentary that may be helpful: "What did God have in mind when He wanted to meet with humans? The Hebrew word for meet is ya'adh, meaning to appoint, fix (a time or place); to give in marriage; to meet by agreement, come together."[1]

When God states His desire to meet with you, He's not talking about two friends casually chatting over coffee. He describes intimacy like that of marriage.

Read Leviticus 26:11-13.

Where did God choose to dwell?

_____

Sins severe fellowship.

Tabernacle = dwelling place

[1] Moore, Beth. A Woman's Heart: God's Dwelling Place (Nashville: LifeWay Press, 1996), 11.

Isn't it interesting that even though the Garden of Eden still existed, God chose not to stay there. He could have continued to take His evening walks there in quiet peace without the noise of the bumbling humans. Where did God choose to walk instead?

❑ on Mt. Sinai   ❑ in the wilderness
❑ Jerusalem   ❑ among the Israelites

Read Micah 6:8.

In this verse, God clearly states what He desires from you during your life on earth. Write these three things below:

1. _____

2. _____

3. _____

You may be wondering by now, "If I'm supposed to walk with God, where are we going together?" This Hebrew word for walk, halak, is very interesting. It means "to walk. . .with or without any suggestion of a definite destination. It is also used figuratively to denote one's lifestyle, as well as an individual's continuing relationship with God."²

As far as God is concerned, the destination is not all that important. What matters to God is the walk itself. . .just sharing fellowship along the road. This is God's great passion for you. He continues to express this desire all through the Old Testament. During the wilderness wanderings, God inhabited the tabernacle, a portable temple. Eventually, God led them into the Promised Land where the Israelites would make their home. When Solomon built the temple (1 Kings 7), God dwelled among His people in that place as well.

The major problem with this arrangement was the limited access between God and His people. Read Hebrews 9:6-7 below, which describe the activities in the earthly tabernacle.

When everything had been arranged like this, the priests entered regularly into the outer room to carry on their ministry. But only the high priest entered the inner room, and that only once a year, and never without blood, which he offered for himself and for the sins the people had committed in ignorance.

Who was allowed access to the presence of God?

_____

God was not satisfied with this arrangement, which only allowed the priests to be close to Him. He wanted a deeper relationship with normal people like you. So read further in Hebrews 10:19-22 to see what God did.

² Hebrew Greek Key Study Bible, NIV, AMG International, Inc., 1996, p.1512.

Therefore, brothers, since we have confidence to enter the Most Holy Place by the blood of Jesus, by a new and living way open for us through the curtain, that is, his body, and since we have a great priest over the house of God, let us draw near to God with a sincere heart with full assurance of faith, having our hearts sprinkled to cleanse us from a guilty conscience and having our bodies washed with pure water.

Do you remember what happened to the curtain, or veil, in the temple when Jesus died? It was torn in two. In verse 20, what other "curtain" was opened so that we might enter the Most Holy Place?

_____

Do you understand what this means? Intimate fellowship with God is not reserved for priests, youth ministers, pastors, and super-spiritual believers. God threw open the door and said, "I want you to come meet with me!"

What does verse 22 say we are supposed to do, then?

❑ Run away   ❑ Draw near   ❑ Be afraid

God desires nothing more that for you to draw near to Him. He wants this so badly that He doesn't even live within brick walls or temple gates (Acts 17:24).

Write out 1 Corinthians 3:16 below.

_____

_____

God has a new dwelling place. Your heart is as close as He could possibly get to share fellowship with you. He made it possible for you not to have to go to any particular building to meet with Him. He invites you, anytime, anyplace, just to sit down and say "hello."

DAY 5 SUMMARY

- God passionately desires to meet with you.
- Walking with God is a journey more than it is destination.

Write your own prayer here.

_____

_____

_____

_____

God says, "I want to meet with you."

WEEK 7

Spiritual Fitness—Diet

Week 7:

SPIRITUAL FITNESS — DIET

Who watches infomercials? The average 30-second commercial is enough to drive you crazy; why would anyone want to sit down and watch a 30-minute commercial? The ironic part is that most of these TV time-wasters are trying to sell products for health and fitness to people sitting on a couch eating potato chips! Some infomercials try to convince people that diet is the key to staying healthy. "Eat our products and drink our protein malts (not to be confused with a delicious ice cream milkshake), and you will stay fit and trim." Other infomercials sing the praises of the next, new exercise machine. "You can walk/ride/fly your way to the body you've always wanted!" What a joke! Ask any fitness expert who is not paid to sell a product this question: "What will it take for me to stay in good physical condition?" The answer will be the same: "Diet and exercise." To stay healthy, you must eat right and stay physically active.

The same thing is true for you spiritually. Nothing is more important in the upcoming transition than for you to maintain a healthy faith. This includes both your spiritual diet and your spiritual exercise. The rest of this study focuses on these two factors for your spiritual wellness. This week you will concentrate on Christian nourishment—the "intake" which provides strength and endurance. Next week you will shift focus to spiritual exercise - the "output" through which God builds His Kingdom on earth.

Day 1 Quiet Time Redefined
Day 2 Beyond the Menu
Day 3 Enjoying the Meal
Day 4 Disciplined Encounters
Day 5 Creative Encounters

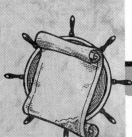

MEMORY VERSE FOR THE WEEK

Hebrews 11:6
"For without faith it is impossible to please God, because anyone who comes to him must believe that he exists and that he rewards those who earnestly seek him."

DAY 1: QUIET TIME REDEFINED

From Day Five of your study last week, what can you say for sure that God desires?

God wants _____.

God threw open the door and extended the invitation for you to enter a Holy Place where only the high priest could go before. In this inner sanctuary, God makes His residence today.

According to 1 Corinthians 3:16, where does God dwell?

_____

Sometimes school can be really frustrating, especially when you're studying at home and the textbook is unclear. The teacher, who expects you to understand what you are reading, is not there to explain the text to you. You never have this problem with God. You are in God's presence right now, even as you read this workbook. If you haven't done this already, stop and acknowledge that He is with you in this moment. The Teacher who knows everything stands ready to help you understand!

You are in God's presence — right now!

Maybe you have responded to the invitation to meet with God in the past. You most likely have heard a Quiet Time explained as a time that you spend alone with God. Praying, reading Scripture, or going through a devotional book are a few of the activities you might have tried. Mark an X on the line below the word that accurately describes your experience with Quiet Times so far as a Christian.

◄──►

daily   most days   hit or miss   rarely   never

Surely one of the largest barriers to spending time alone with God is knowing what to do when you get there. Let's establish a reasonable goal for a Quiet Time. God says He wants to meet with you. From Day Five of last week, what words describe what God has in mind when He uses the word "meets"?

❏ study facts   ❏ meet by agreement
❏ come together   ❏ think out loud
❏ fix a time or place   ❏ give in marriage

By using these phrases you can put together a definition that sounds like this.

Quiet Time: To come together with God by agreement at a fixed time and place to share intimate (marriage-like) fellowship.

Read the passage below from Jeremiah 9:23-24.

This is what the Lord says: "Let not the wise man boast of his wisdom or the strong man boast of his strength or the rich man boast of his riches, but let him who boasts boast about this: that he understands and knows me, that I am the Lord, who exercises kindness, justice and righteousness on earth, for in these I delight," declares the Lord.

In the passage above, circle the words that describe things people boast about. You can identify people like this at your school in a heartbeat. Some students quickly tell you about the test they aced or about the latest scholarship they received. Some athletes brag on and on about the last game or how much weight they can lift. And what is more obnoxious than someone who tries to impress others with their money or material possessions? Intellect, strength, and riches hold little value compared with what God really desires.

In the above passage what two things matter most to God?

_____ and _____

When was the last time you felt misunderstood? Sometimes parents come to quick conclusions and don't even listen to the full story. Friends can act the same way. God wants you to understand Him, and to know that He understands you. The Hebrew word used here for "understand" means to comprehend, or to gain insight into someone else. Your intellect is not worth boasting about unless it is used to understand the Creator.

In addition to wanting you to understand Him, God also says He wants you to know Him. This Hebrew word "yada" encompasses even the most intimate form of sexual union. Certainly, God's character goes beyond our ability to comprehend Him fully, but this word means that we relate on a personal level with the True God.

Review the stated definition of a Quiet Time again.

> To come together with God by agreement at a fixed time and place to share intimate (marriage-like) fellowship.

During your previous Quiet Times you may have attempted to study about God, hoping to pick up a nugget of Truth about Him. But knowing about someone and really knowing someone can be very different. Christian communicator Louie Giglio suggests the following exercise as a way for you to understand the difference. In the box below, write the name of the most nationally famous person you know about who is alive today. It could be a politician, sports figure, or other celebrity. Then write down a few facts *about* that person.

FAMOUS PERSON:

_____

facts:

So when was the last time you spent the day with that person? Does he call you often to chat about his life? Or maybe she stopped by last week because she was in the neighborhood. While you might have a close relationship with someone famous, most people just know about them. Rarely does intimate knowledge exist between a celebrity and a fan. You probably don't share quiet, relaxed moments where the conversation ends and you sit silently and comfortably in each other's presence.

The same may be true between you and God. You may know more about God than you actually know Him. Far too many Christians believe the goal of a Quiet Time is to gain information about God. In reality, your goal is to relate to Him, experience Him, and know Him.

Write out Psalm 34:8 in the blanks below:

_____

_____

Which word describes the activity in this verse?

❏ Study   ❏ Think   ❏ Smell
❏ Memorize   ❏ Taste   ❏ Train

God desires for you to move beyond studying Him. He wants you to taste His goodness. You can learn about being forgiven, but when you feel guilty you need to taste forgiveness. You can theologically understand that God is wise, but when your circumstances leave you completely confused you need to taste of His wisdom. You might know in your head that your life is valuable, but when you feel worthless and insignificant you need to taste the true worth that God gives you. Maybe you know that God is everywhere, but when you feel completely lonely, you need more than information; you need to *taste* of His constant companionship.

In the list below, check one or more ways that you need a taste of God's goodness today.

❏ forgiveness   ❏ perspective

❏ companionship   ❏ joy and pleasure

❏ worth and value   ❏ integrity

❏ leadership   ❏ friendship

❏ wisdom   ❏ peace

❏ hope   ❏ acceptance

❏ other _____   ❏ other _____

Knowing about
$\neq$
knowing

Taste and see that God is good.

151

As you complete today's study, keep Psalm 34:8 in mind. This verse opens a door to consider the Scriptural image of hunger and food. You will pick up with this concept tomorrow. Finish today by reading Matthew 5:6.

What is the promise offered to those who hunger and thirst for righteousness?

_____

_____

In your closing prayer today, write some thoughts about your spiritual hunger to know God. Honestly state your goal of knowing Him personally. As you prayerfully write, remain aware than He is right beside you reading every word.

DAY 1 SUMMARY

- A Quiet Time is a meeting with God.
- God desires that you know Him, not just know about Him.

Write your own prayer here.

_____

_____

_____

_____

_____

_____

DAY 2: BEYOND THE MENU

Before you being today's study, prayerfully state your desire to meet with God and know Him personally. Write this week's memory verse below.

Hebrews 11:6

_____

_____

_____

Today you will look at some very practical activities to help build intimacy in your relationship with God. In the box below, write some things you might do when alone with God.

```




```

Imagine being extremely hungry. You have gone for several days without food, and now you are starving for nourishment. You choose a place like Denny's or Shoney's because you know it will meet your gnawing hunger pangs. As you look over the menu, you see pictures of entrees and begin to salivate. The room fills with delicious smells which make your stomach ache with anticipation. On the back of the menu you pore over the dessert selections, savoring every word of the detailed descriptions. When the server arrives to take your order, you close the menu, hand it to him and say, "No thank you. I've had enough."

What?! That's completely ridiculous. Why would any hungry person go to a restaurant, look at the menu, smell the cooked food, and choose not to enjoy the meal? That's a good question.

Here is another good question: Why would any spiritually hungry Christian sit down to read the Word of God and not enjoy the God of the Word? If you have a Quiet Time and you do not personally relate to God, you have missed the meal altogether. Some believers wrongly think that reading Scripture is the meal. In truth, Scripture is only the menu. Jesus is the meal. If you read the Bible and miss out on Jesus, you leave your Quiet Time more spiritually hungry than when you first sat down.

Scripture = menu

Jesus = meal

To underscore this point, read John 6:35, 48-51 and fill in the blanks below.

Jesus said He is the _____ of life.

Whoever comes to Him will never go _____.

Whoever believes in Him will never be _____.

What is unique about this bread? _____

What happens to the person who eats living bread?_____

_____

Read the rest of this passage, John 6:52-57.

Then the Jews began to argue sharply among themselves, "How can this man give us his flesh to eat?" Jesus said to them, "I tell you the truth, unless you eat the flesh of the Son of Man and drink his blood, you have no life in you. Whoever eats my flesh and drinks my blood has eternal life, and I will raise him up at the last day. For my flesh is real food and my blood is real drink. Whoever eats my flesh and drinks my blood remains in me, and I in him. Just as the living Father sent me and I live because of the Father, so the one who feeds on me will live because of me.

Jesus says believers are supposed to _____ Him.

❑ talk to   ❑ pray to   ❑ sing about
❑ feed on   ❑ worship   ❑ tell others about

Jesus has not lost His mind. He knows people will not literally eat His flesh or drink His blood. In verse 63, He explains that He is referring to spiritual rather than physical matters. You experience this hunger and thirst on a spirit level, and it cannot be relieved by anything physical. Rather, your needs are met in the context of a relationship.

When was the last time you had a deeply meaningful conversation with someone? What made that time special for you?

```
┌─────────────────────────────────────────────────────────┐
│                                                           │
│                                                           │
│                                                           │
│                                                           │
│                                                           │
└─────────────────────────────────────────────────────────┘
```

Relationships nourish the soul.

Relationships nourish the soul. A meaningful conversation fills you with warmth and confidence. Compliments from a special friend feed your self-esteem. Encouragement renews your strength. Like food nourishes your body, relationships nourish your spirit.

Write out John 6:63 in the blanks below.

_____

_____

Jesus wants you to feed on Him. The nourishment He offers is not for the stomach, but for the spirit. If you relate to Jesus as He desires, your life will be filled to satisfaction. You will experience joy and pleasure this world can't supply. Your strength will endure through the most difficult times. You can know peace and contentment about your future. Your relationship with Christ will bring to your life a sense of purpose that extends eternally beyond graduation, college, marriage, or a career.

Read John 7:37-39.

Who was speaking? _____

When did this take place? _____

What were thirsty people supposed to do? _____

What results from believing in Christ? _____

Because the Holy Spirit lives in your heart by faith, you have a constant flow of all you need for abundant, holy life. As 2 Peter 1:3 says, "His divine power has given us everything we need for life and godliness *through our knowledge of him* who called us by his own glory and goodness" (italics added). Notice where everything you need is found: through the knowledge of God. You no longer need to search for fulfillment in the world. In fact, since the wellspring flows from within you, you now have life-giving water to offer others who are spiritually dying of thirst. Proverbs 10:21 says, "The lips of the righteous nourish many. . . ."

In the past you may have depended heavily on the lips of others to provide spiritual nourishment for you. Now you see that Jesus can provide what you need directly. Tomorrow you will learn a Bible study technique that equips you with the necessary utensils to enjoy the spiritual feast.

DAY 2 SUMMARY

- Scripture is the menu; Jesus is the meal.
- Those who feed on Jesus are fulfilled.
- Your relationship with Him nourishes your spirit.

Write your own prayer here.

_____

_____

_____

_____

_____

DAY 3: ENJOYING THE MEAL

It's 6:30 AM. The sound of your alarm worms its way into your cocoon of sweet dreams and cozy covers. You try to block out the noise, but to no avail. Finally, you drag your weary bones out of bed and begin your morning routine. By 7:15, you are ready to have a Quiet Time. The Bible reading you've chosen for the day is 1 John 4. You fight off the urge to take a quick nap, and you begin to study. Before too long, your mom's loud banging on the door jolts you awake for the second time. And you've had yet another less than meaningful Quiet Time.

Has this ever happened to you? Maybe this has happened to you so many times that you've all but given up Scripture reading in the morning. The problem is not your Bible or your good intentions to grow in faith. The real problem may be your focus.

Remember the goal of a Quiet Time from Day One of this week. Write it down in the blanks below.

_____

_____

If you set out merely to read the Bible, you may quickly grow weary. But if your objective is to meet with God, you will remain keenly alert.

Let's use 1 John 4:10 to illustrate a Bible study method that will get you off the pages of Scripture and into the presence of God.[1] As you use this technique, you will move beyond the menu and begin to enjoy the meal.

The basic premise of this method is that you can read Scripture four different ways. The following guide will walk you through these four perspectives one at a time.

1 GENERALLY

First, you can read Scripture *generally*. When you read a verse generally, you are reading it as it is written on the page.

1 John 4:10
This is love: not that we loved God, but that he loved us and sent his Son as an atoning sacrifice for our sins.

At this point, you may or may not understand the meaning of this verse. Sometimes reading Scripture can feel as impersonal as reading a history textbook. Notice that the writer uses the words "we" and "us." He writes these words to all who follow Jesus Christ by faith. In fact, the whole Bible is God's personal message for all believers. So, as an individual believer, you can say, "If it's written for Christians, it's written for me personally."

2 PERSONALLY

Secondly, you can read Scripture *personally*. When you read a verse this way, you are reading it as if it were written just about you.

1 John 4:10
*This is love: not that **I** loved God, but that he loved **me** and sent his Son as an atoning sacrifice for **my** sins.*

By changing the pronouns from "we" and "us" to "me" and "I" you gain a new sense of personal relevance. If you consider the Bible as important just for the church, you may bypass its personal message for you as an individual follower of Christ. Possibly you have tried this technique in the past, putting your name in John 3:16. "For God so loved me. . ." But if you stop here, you may still miss the meal in this encounter with God.

[1] Louie Giglio. "The Spiral of Sin and Temptation" (Atlanta: Choice Ministries, Inc.).

For the word of God is living and active. Sharper than any double-edged sword, it penetrates even to dividing soul and spirit, joints and marrow; it judges the thoughts and attitudes of the heart.

Hebrews 4:12

③ RELATIONALLY

Thirdly, you can read Scripture *relationally*. When you read a verse this way, you are reading it as a prayer to God.

1 John 4:10
This is love: not that I loved you, but that you loved me and sent your Son as an atoning sacrifice for my sins.

Stop right here, and look closely at the critical step you are taking. When you read the Bible you are looking at a page, but when you *pray* the Bible, you are looking at God. By approaching Scripture relationally, you move from reading to relating. Now this is more than a study — it is a conversation! You might even find that each phrase produces a spontaneous prayer.

"This is love, (and I really want to know how to define love in this world, God. Friendships and dating can leave me confused about genuine love.)"

"Not that I loved you (for my love of you is fickle. Sometimes I love you dearly. Other times I deny that I know you at all. My love is not a good definition of love.)"

"But that you loved me (unconditionally, willingly, and sacrificially. Your love is pure and holy. You love me because you made me. Thank you God for defining love accurately.)"

Many Christians gets distracted when praying silently. Praying a verse helps to maintain your focus. Reading Scripture relationally keeps your mind on track; it is your springboard into a meaningful conversation with God.

④ REFLECTIVELY

Fourth, you can read Scripture *reflectively*. When you read a verse this way, you are reading it as God's voice speaking directly to you.

1 John 4:10
*This is love: not that you loved **me**, but that **I** loved **you** and sent **my** Son as an atoning sacrifice for **your** sins.*

Have you ever heard someone say, "God spoke to me today"? How did you feel when you heard this?

```



```

Listen for God's voice!

Maybe you thought, "Oh really? What did He sound like?" or "Sure, as if God would really say something to you directly. Who do you think you are, Moses?" Or "Wow, I wonder if God might speak to me, too." God speaks clearly to His people every day. His voice sounds just like His Word. When you read Scripture as a prayer, God bounces His Word back like an echo from heaven. His voice is a mirror reflection of His Word. Next time you read Scripture, listen closely for the gentle whisper—or rolling thunder—of God's voice.

The end result of this technique lines up the definition of the word "yada"—to meet with God.

Now it's time for you to work through this technique with a different verse. Start with a simple prayer: "God I want to hear your voice as I read your Word."

Write out Ephesians 1:4 **Generally** (just like it's written on the page).

_____

_____

Now, rewrite Ephesians 1:4 **Personally** (changing the words "us" and "we" to "me" and "I").

_____

_____

Write Ephesians 1:4 **Relationally** (as a prayer from your heart to God). Take some time with this one. Tell God how you feel about being chosen to be in Christ.

_____

_____

_____

_____

_____

Finally, write Ephesians 1:4 **Reflectively** (the way it would sound if God said it just to you).

_____

_____

"Yada" = to meet with God

Can you remember a time in your life when you were not chosen? You probably felt rejected, turned down, or not good enough. The God of the universe just made a bold statement to you. Read it again slowly. Congratulations! Regardless of the world's evaluation, God chose you! Now you are hearing the voice of God.

Finish today by trying this method with one of your favorite verses. Sometimes, a verse may already be written personally or relationally. If so, make that verse your personal prayer.

Verse: _____

Generally:

_____

_____

_____

Personally:

_____

_____

_____

_____

_____

Relationally:

_____

_____

_____

_____

Reflectively:

_____

_____

_____

My sheep listen to my voice; I know them and they follow me.

John 10:27

If you want to be a Christian who truly meets with God, learn God's Word. As Louie Giglio states it, "He who knows God's Word the best, hears God's voice the most."

In your closing prayer, thank God for meeting with you today.

DAY 3 SUMMARY

- Meeting with God in Scripture means more than reading the words on the page.
- God's voice sounds just like His Word.
- "He who knows God's Word the best, hears God's voice the most."

Write your own prayer here.

_____

_____

_____

_____

_____

DAY 4: DISCIPLINED ENCOUNTERS

Today you will examine several other doorways through which you can experience God. Some of these may sound basic to you, but don't gloss over them too quickly. You may find that some old habits lead to fresh encounters with God.

Consider this illustration.

A man left home for a long journey. He packed his bags and locked up the house. Knowing he wouldn't be able to water his plants for several weeks, he put all four on the back porch and hoped for the best.

When he arrived safely home, he found the house still in good shape. But on the porch, something odd had happened. Two of the plants were completely dead while the other two looked better than ever. Confused and curious, he left them outside to see if the mystery would solve itself. The next day it began to rain. Through the window, the man saw what unlocked the mystery. The two dead plants sat sheltered under the rooftop. Not more than a drop of rain touched their dry soil. The healthy plants, on the other hand, caught the rain running off the drainspout. They lived and grew. The only difference between these two plants and the other two plants was where they were sitting.

Now picture two college freshmen sitting in their dorm room, both having a Quiet Time. Both are reading Scripture. Both are writing thoughts in a journal. Both are reading a daily devotional book. These students are doing the exact same things. One of them, feeling as spiritually dry as the desert, struggles to find purpose or value in those activities. The other student feels invigorated, like taking a refreshing drink from a spiritual fountain. This freshman is ready to meet the challenges of a new day with heavenly strength.

What's the difference? The first student is just sitting in the dorm room. The second one is sitting in the presence of God. Like the plants, the only difference between the two is where they were sitting. Quiet Time activities can be as boring as homework, or as exciting as climbing a mountain. The difference is not in your activities, but God's presence in the midst of them.

As you meet with God you will engage in various spiritual disciplines such as Bible reading, praying, meditating, and journaling. Kept in proper perspective, these disciplines can place you in the full flow of God's abundant presence.

Author and teacher Richard Foster describes spiritual disciplines this way:

> A farmer is helpless to grow grain; all he can do is provide the right conditions for the growing of grain. He puts the seed in the ground where the natural forces take over and up comes the grain. That is the way with the Spiritual Disciplines—they are a way of sowing to the Spirit. The Disciplines are God's way of getting us into the ground; they put us where He can work within us and transform us. By themselves the Spiritual Disciplines can do nothing; they can only get us to the place where something can be done. . . .God has ordained the Disciplines of the spiritual life as the means by which we are placed where He can bless us.[1]

Read the following verses and record the common theme.

Psalm 16:11

Psalm 21:6

Acts 2:28

Common theme:_____

To experience the joy of the Lord, you must sit, as Mary did, in the presence of Jesus. Spiritual disciplines have no power to produce joy on their own, but they can place you before the One who can. Now let's look at the disciplines individually.

[1] Richard Foster. Celebration of Discipline (San Francisco: Harper & Row, Publishers, Inc., 1978), 6.

1. BIBLE READING

Yesterday you learned a Scripture reading technique that allows you to relate more personally to God. If you desire to enter an intimate relationship with God, the Bible is the doorway. The only way to know the God of the Word is to faithfully read the Word of God.

Before theologian David Watson died of cancer he wrote these words:

> As I spent time chewing over the endless assurances and promises to be found in the Bible, so my faith in the living God grew stronger and held me safe in his hands. God's word to us, especially his word spoken by his Spirit through the Bible, is the very ingredient that feeds our faith. If we feed our souls regularly on God's word, several times each day, we should become robust spiritually just as we feed on ordinary food several times each day, and become robust physically. Nothing is more important than hearing and obeying the word of God.[2]

Draw a line matching these verses to the corresponding description of the Word of God.

Psalm 119:105	The Word is flawless.
Proverbs 30:5	The Word is a sword.
Hebrews 4:12	The Word is a lamp.
John 17:17	The Word is Truth.

If you attend college, the course of your entire education will require you to read many textbooks. All this reading will prepare you to take tests and pass classes. God provided you a single Textbook for life. The Bible prepares you to pass all of life's tests, and it reveals to you the One who gives the passing grade.

2. PRAYING

Now look at another spiritual discipline: prayer. If you pray like the first freshman in the story, unaware of God's presence, you are basically thinking out loud. Praying to God makes your talking out loud a meaningful conversation.

Read Mark 1:35.

Where did Jesus go? _____

When did Jesus go? _____

What did Jesus do? _____

[2] David Watson. Fear No Evil: A Personal Struggle with Cancer (London: Hodder and Stoughton, 1984), 39.

"Nothing is more important than hearing and obeying the Word of God."

— Richard Foster

When you pray, follow Jesus' example. Find a solitary place at a time free from distractions. Pray out loud so that your mind stays focused.

Think about the best time and place for you to regularly meet with God.

MY REGULAR MEETING WITH GOD

When: _____

Where: _____

Bishop Fenelon describes prayer as an honest, familiar conversation between friends:

> *Tell God all that is in your heart, as one unloads one's heart, its pleasures and its pains to a dear friend. Tell him your troubles, that he may comfort you; tell him your joys, that he may sober them; tell him your longings, that he may purify them; tell him your dislikes, that the may help you conquer them; talk to him of your temptations, that he may shield you from them; show him the wounds of your heart, that he may heal them; lay bear your indifference to good, your depraved tastes for evil, your instability. Tell him how self-love makes you unjust to others, how vanity tempts you to be insincere, how pride disguises you to yourself and others. If you thus pour out all your weaknesses, needs, troubles, there will be no lack of what to say. You will never exhaust the subject. It is continually being renewed. People who have no secrets from each other never want for subjects of conversation. They do not weigh their words, for there is nothing to be held back; neither do they seek for something to say. They talk out of the abundance of the heart, without consideration they say just what they think. Blessed are they who attain to such familiar, unreserved [interaction] with God.[3]*

Do you approach prayer in this way? Why or why not?

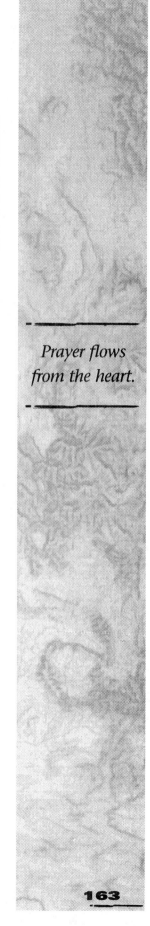

Prayer flows from the heart.

Entire study courses focus on the topics of Bible study and prayer. But the best way to learn how to pray is to do it. If you have trouble concentrating because things you need to do keep popping into your head, write those things on a "to do" list and get back to praying. Use Scripture as a tool to generate your prayers. Don't worry about proper religious words. Just pour out your heart to the One who cares to listen.

[3] Francois Fenelon. Quoted in Chuck Swindoll. Reflections from the Heart (Anaheim, CA: Insight for Living, 1993.) For more readings by Francois Fenelon, see Talking with God (Brewster, MA: Paraclete Press, 1997).

3. MEDITATING

Now for the third discipline today: meditation. This one may be less familiar to you. Maybe you picture a group of bald Buddhist monks chanting mystic meditations. Or maybe you imagine someone sitting up straight with legs crossed and hands on their knees, eyes closed, and humming. For Christians, meditation is not some mysterious New Age or Eastern technique. In fact, meditation has a biblical basis.

Read Genesis 24:63.

What was Isaac doing?

_____

What was the Psalmist meditating on in the following verses?

Psalm 48:9 _____

Psalm 77:12 _____

Psalm 119:27 _____

Psalm 119:148 _____

Eastern meditation tries to empty the mind of all thoughts. Christian meditation seeks to fill the mind with thoughts of God. In a very real sense, meditating is nothing more than concentrated thinking. When you mentally "chew" on a problem or a Scripture passage, you're meditating.

Richard Foster adds this perspective:

> Some shy away from meditation out of fear that it is too difficult, too complicated. Perhaps it is best left to the professional who has more time to explore the inner regions. Not at all. . . .Anyone who can tap the power of the imagination can learn to meditate. If we are capable of listening to our dreams, we are taking the first steps.[4]

Now let's practice this spiritual discipline:

Write out Psalm 26:2-3 in the blanks below.

_____

_____

_____

_____

Christian meditation fills your mind with thoughts of God.

[4] Foster, op. cit., p.16.

Read each line again slowly. Think about what it means. "Chew" on ways this verse might apply to your life. Record your reflections in the box below.

4. JOURNALING

The last of the disciplines mentioned in this study is journaling. Congratulations! If you've been writing in the thought boxes and recording your prayers at the end of each day, you have been journaling. Hopefully this study has helped you form a habit of recording what you are saying to God and what He is communicating to you.

DAY 4 SUMMARY

Spiritual disciplines can't produce joy, but they can place you in the presence of the One who can.

Write your own prayer here.

_____

_____

_____

_____

_____

DAY 5: CREATIVE ENCOUNTERS

Today's study will introduce you to several more doorways through which you can enter God's presence. Write the memory verse below.

Hebrews 11:6

_____

_____

_____

As you begin, write a prayer acknowledging God's presence with you and your desire to know Him during this meeting.

_____

_____

_____

Relationships demand creativity. Imagine a dating relationship where you do the same thing every time you are with that person. Each date looks exactly like the last one, and you know the next one will be no different. After a while, you would surely grow weary and beg to do something else. Variety and spontaneity are parts of a healthy dating relationship. It's no different in your relationship with God. While He never tires of your disciplined spiritual activities, you do. To stay fresh, interested and engaged with God, you may need to vary your approach occasionally.

Below you will find a list of ideas for creative encounters with God. After you read them, choose one and try it today. Allow yourself at least 20 minutes to complete the activity, and remember that relating to God is your foremost purpose.

1. **Private worship.** Pick one of your favorite hymns or choruses. Write down the words and pray through each line. Look up verses that support the lyrics. Finish by singing the song just to God.

2. **Tracking God.** Few people are good at keeping a daily journal. However, you should not commit the same mistakes of the Israelites, who forgot what the Lord had done on their behalf. Think of several ways you have seen God move powerfully, such that you know He was at work. Write them down. On days when God seems to be far away and your faith is wavering, you can read the accounts of how He demonstrated His love in the past.

3. **Audio devo.** Pick a song from a Christian artist who writes lyrics based on Scripture. Listen to the song a few times then do a Bible study based on the theme. Look up related verses. Spend some time considering how that song might minister to you in certain situations.

4. **Active reading.** Pick up a Christian book that relates to a spiritual topic. Read a chapter slowly. Look up the Scripture references to see if you can draw the same conclusions as the author. Pray in constant dialogue with God as you read.

5. **Prayer walk.** Go out for a walk with God, enjoying His creation with Him. Remain mindful of His presence as you go. Let your conversation with Him reflect what you are experiencing along the way.

6. **Private service.** During a private moment of devotion, you might feel led to do something that anonymously meets someone else's need. Pray as you serve that your friend will be blessed simply by knowing that somebody cared.

7. **Written devo.** If you expresses yourself best in writing, use that ability to write a poem, hymn, chorus, or letter to God. Let it reflect the overflow of your heart.

Now it's your turn. Pick one of the suggestions above and go meet with God. He eagerly waits for you to join Him in fellowship.

DAY 5 SUMMARY

• Variety helps you stay engaged in the pursuit of God.

MY CREATIVE ENCOUNTER

_____

_____

_____

_____

_____

_____

_____

_____

_____

_____

_____

_____

_____

_____

_____

_____

_____

_____

_____

_____

_____

_____

_____

_____

_____

_____

_____

_____

_____

_____

_____

_____

_____

_____

_____

_____

_____

_____

_____

_____

_____

_____

_____

_____

_____

_____

_____

_____

_____

_____

_____

_____

_____

_____

_____

_____

_____

_____

WEEK 8

Spiritual Fitness
— Exercise

Week 8:

SPIRITUAL FITNESS — EXERCISE

Do you realize what you've done? Not only have you made it to the last week of this study, you have also increased the probability that you will successfully make the spiritual transition from high school to beyond. Try to imagine yourself living away from home, but enjoying the company of God's presence. As last week's memory verse states, "He rewards those who earnestly seek Him." God's rewards come in many forms. He grants the rewards of contentment and perspective. He rewards you with his leadership for your future. But most importantly, He rewards you by revealing Himself to you. When Abraham wondered if God would ever grant him a son, God responded, "Do not be afraid, Abram. I am your shield, your very great reward" (Genesis 15:1).

In Week Seven you studied the importance of your meeting times with God. If you neglect these divine appointments, you forfeit the reward of knowing God. But if you encounter God personally, face to face, your whole life is flooded with enthusiasm that can't be constrained. So, then, what do you do with all this excitement? *Express your faith in acts of service.* God works miracles in your life so that He can bless others through your life. The last week of this study focuses on this theme: Working out your faith. A healthy diet is the first step. Now it's time to exercise.

Day 1 Devoted to Good

Day 2 Big Church

Day 3 Made for Ministry

Day 4 A Servant's Heart

Day 5 The Expedition

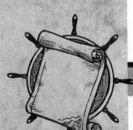

MEMORY PASSAGE FOR THE WEEK:

Matthew 5:14-16
"You are the light of the world. A city on a hill cannot be hidden. Neither do people light a lamp and put it under a bowl. Instead they put it on its stand, and it gives light to everyone in the house. In the same way, let your light shine before men, that they may see your good deeds and praise your Father in heaven."

DAY 1: DEVOTED TO GOOD

For two weeks you have considered the importance of meeting with God. Encountering Him through the Word is your primary means of spiritual nourishment. By nurturing your relationship with God, you spiritually ingest "solid food" which helps you to mature. But ingestion is only one step in the process.

You may have heard of the eating disorder, bulimia. More than just a dietary problem, it can be life-threatening. A person who suffers from bulimia eats, sometimes even gorging on food. But then the bulimic person expels the food before it has a chance to digest. In the end, her body wastes away from lack of essential nutrients. The bulimic person engages in a dangerous form of deception. She thinks that by eating, her body will benefit, when in fact she gradually robs herself of everything beneficial. The food is ingested, but it is not digested. This same disorder can apply to your walk with God.

Read James 1:22-25.

What deception is described in verse 22?

_____

_____

You may be tempted, like the bulimic individual, to think that ingestion is the key to health. You listen to sermons, read your Bible, and pay attention in Sunday School. Isn't that enough? Not even close! After spiritual ingestion comes spiritual digestion. To get a practical definition of spiritual digestion, write out the rest of this verse below.

Do not merely listen to the word, and so deceive yourselves.

_____

Digestion bridges the gap between meditation and application. If meditation causes the Word to sink into your heart, application causes the Word to spring out of your life. Go all the way back to Week One, Day Two of the workbook and find the phrase that completes this sentence:

Your behavior doesn't determine your identity, but _____

_____

According to the passage in James, if you listen to the Word and don't apply it, you are like a man who forgets his identity. But if you allow the Word to digest in your soul, it will become outwardly visible to everyone you encounter.

To digest the Word, apply it.

Read Titus 3:3-7 below.

At one time we too were foolish, disobedient, deceived and enslaved by all kinds of passions and pleasures. We lived in malice and envy, being hated and hating one another. But when the kindness and love of God our Savior appeared, he saved us, not because of righteous things we had done, but because of his mercy. He saved us through the washing of rebirth and renewal by the Holy Spirit, whom he poured out on us generously through Jesus Christ our Savior, so that having been justified by his grace, we might become heirs having the hope of eternal life.

What is Paul talking about in these verses?

❏ Salvation in Christ   ❏ Suffering
❏ Temptation   ❏ Missions

Now read verse 8:

This is a trustworthy saying. And I want you to stress these things, so that those who have trusted in God may be careful to devote themselves to doing what is good. These things are excellent and profitable for everyone.

Why does Paul say he wants these things to be stressed?

_____

_____

Good works bring God pleasure.

In the Christian life, good works naturally flow from understanding what God has done for you. These good things are not only part of God's plan, they bring Him pleasure.

What are the two words Paul uses to describe the good things Christians do?

_____ and _____

Read and match the following verses which elaborate the value of doing good.

_____ 1 Peter 2:12   A. Good deeds fulfill God's purpose for you.

_____ Titus 2:14   B. Good deeds shine like light.

_____ Matthew 5:16   C. Good deeds show enthusiasm for God.

_____ Ephesians 2:10   D. Good deeds inspire praise in others.

Some people claim that Christianity is a private matter for each individual to personally pursue. While it is true that everyone has to make a personal decision about God, all Christians are charged with the command: In light of who you are, go out and do good! Your life is a public display of your private devotion to God.

What are some ways you publicly display your faith today?

God has given you an outlet through which to express these good deeds: the church. Tomorrow, you will explore what the Bible has to say about church.

Finish today by thanking the Lord for the good things He has done for you. Then ask Him to reveal the good things you can do for Him.

DAY 1 SUMMARY

- Spiritual ingestion is only part of the Christian life; spiritual digestion completes the process of mature faith.

- Good works naturally flow from a heart devoted to God

Write your own prayer here.

_____

_____

_____

_____

_____

DAY 2: BIG CHURCH

Begin today by writing out the memory passage for this week.

Matthew 5:14-16

_____

_____

_____

_____

_____

_____

_____

Today you will do a Bible study on the church. Whether you grew up going to church or have never joined a church fellowship, today's study is designed to broaden your understanding of the church's vital role in the Kingdom of God.

The Bible uses several illustrations to depict the church. Look up these passages and record the Scriptural picture:

Scripture Passage	Scriptural Picture:
2 Corinthians 6:17-18	
1 Corinthians 12:12-13, 27	
Ephesians 2:19-22	
Ephesians 5:25-32	

Your church is one tile in God's mosaic around the world.

The Church[1] is a non-negotiable part of the Christian experience. When you accepted Christ as your Lord, you were automatically placed into the Church. You are now a child in God's family. You are a part of the Body of Christ. You form a brick in God's building project. You are adorned as Christ's bride in eternal marriage.

These pictures illustrate that you have a place in the larger scheme of the Church. Even if you don't always enjoy the experience of a local church, God decided to make Himself known through the Church worldwide. The Church

[1] The word Church is capitalized when referring to the collection of believers around the world.

reveals the greatness of God and serves as His hands and feet on earth. You must come to see church as more than a place you go on Sundays. Your local church is but one tile in God's global mosaic which is the Church universal. While you are member of the universal Church, the local church is your outlet to express the enthusiasm you feel for God. Church opens a door for you to perform the good deeds God has prepared for you.

Unfortunately, many high school graduates place low value on the church. Many drop out and use the time to do other things. But the more you earnestly seek God, the more He will lead you to invest your time in the church.

Take a few minutes to describe the feelings you have about the church you currently attend. What do you enjoy the most? What keeps you coming back?

Some high school graduates never join a local church after they leave home. They feel so loyal to the church they are leaving that becoming a member somewhere else feels like an act of treason. Plus, what other church has all the positive elements of the one you attended at home?

Many young adults fall into a pattern of visiting a different church each week. Some treat church like a "spiritual buffet." "I go to Sunday School here, but I drive to the worship service over there. On Wednesday nights, I go to this third church because the mid-week Bible study is really fun." The "church-hopping" pattern undermines the fundamental purpose of the church. You don't go to a church, or different churches, because of what it does for you. That's a selfish (and childish) way to approach Christianity. Choose to join a church family, to become part of the Body, and to have a place of service. Infants place their needs first. Adults know how to care for others. As long as you operate with the mindset that the church exists to meet your needs, you remain spiritually immature. From Week Six you know that it's time to grow up into adult-like faith. This means shouldering your part of the load in a local church. Now is the time to decide that church membership will be a part of your spiritual transition away from home.

To make this decision more than a good intention, you need to approach it realistically. No two churches are the same. To try to find a church just like the one you are leaving is unreasonable. It is important for you to decide which factors matter most to you in a local church. In the list below, check the elements you find most important.

- ❏ Planned fellowships
- ❏ Strong preaching
- ❏ Good Sunday School program
- ❏ Traditional worship (hymns)
- ❏ Contemporary worship (choruses)
- ❏ Mission trip opportunities
- ❏ Small group studies
- ❏ Structured accountability available
- ❏ Choir options
- ❏ Worship instrument options (i.e. orchestra)
- ❏ Teaching opportunities
- ❏ Missions emphasis
- ❏ Homeless or inner-city ministries
- ❏ Fellowship with older adults
- ❏ Pastoral care (counseling available)
- ❏ Personal discipleship or mentoring
- ❏ Church size (small or large)
- ❏ Denominational affiliation

Now, of the elements you marked, rank the top three in order below.

1. _____

2. _____

3. _____

These three factors matter the most to you in a church home. When you move away, use these as a guide to determine your best church option. Rather than visiting a different church each week, ask around to find out which churches in the area might provide all three elements. Then, visit each of those churches for a month. You will make a wise decision if you attend the same church several weeks in a row. Pray that God would guide you to the best place to invest your life. It's impossible to put a deadline on joining a new church, but as a general rule, this process should take about four months (or one college semester).

Once you sense God's leadership toward a particular church, you have the opportunity to officially join. Again, many students feel like joining a new church somehow betrays their church back home. Nothing could be further from the truth! The man or woman who demonstrates greater loyalty to a local church than to God's church universal has misplaced affection. Joining a new church signifies that your old church has prepared you well for your future.

Depending on your denomination, there are several ways to join a new church. Most churches invite you to join them by a "transfer of letter." You may think this is a very difficult process by which all your old church records (including Sunday School attendance, total tithes and offerings, salt maps from Vacation Bible School, etc.) are packed into a huge crate and shipped to your new church. Wrong! It's as simple as the exchange of two postcards.

Back in the days of the Wild West, bank robbers would move to a small town and immediately join a church to look respectable. Eventually, the church would send a letter back to that person's old church to see if their story matched up. This began the "transfer of a letter." Today, it's no longer a background check. When a person joins a church in this way, two post-cards simply pass in the mail between the old church and the new one. That's all it takes!

Some churches add a new member class or some other procedure for joining. Here is a short list of denominational requirements for joining a church.

Baptist
In addition to the "transfer of letter," most Baptist churches have two other ways for you to join their fellowship—baptism and watchcare.

baptism. Many Baptist churches invite Christians from different denominations to join by baptism. If you are interested in joining a Baptist church for the first time, ask the pastor to explain the symbolic value of being baptized into the church.

watchcare. A growing number of Baptist churches allow people to join by watchcare, which means your "official" membership remains at a former church. In reality, it simply means the churches don't send the postcard!

Methodist
Joining most Methodist churches involves filling out a form and "transferring your letter." Again, it's a matter of postcards in the mail.

Presbyterian
Many Presbyterian churches ask you to attend a New Members Class and transfer your letter. You may have the option of becoming an "affiliate member," which means your home church retains your official "letter" while you attend and serve your local church.

Bible Church/Non-denominational
As a general rule, Bible churches ask new members to attend a Newcomer's Class. Individuals churches may set up their own qualifications for membership.

Assembly of God
To join an Assembly of God church, you would transfer your letter and attend a membership class.

Denomination = a religious organization that unites local congregations

Join a new church within four months!

Episcopalian
Episcopal churches ask for a transfer of letter if you are already a member of an Episcopalian church; if not, you may need to complete a confirmation class.

Lutheran
For many Lutheran churches, joining means you transfer your letter and attend a six-week new member class.

Church of Christ
If you are already a member of the Church of Christ, there is no formal procedure for joining most other churches in this denomination; you just identify with the congregation, letting them know that you'd like to be part of their fellowship. If you are joining from another denomination, talk to the pastor of the local church to get more information.

Certainly, this is not an exhaustive list of churches or denominations; you may choose to join church other than the ones listed above. You will find that individual churches may vary with regard to membership. Whatever one you choose, you rarely will find a church that makes becoming a member difficult.

Finish today by reading Hebrews 10:25.

This verse tells you not to give up

❏ tithing   ❏ Bible study and prayer
❏ serving others   ❏ meeting together

In God's eyes, the church is essential. Why should the church be anything less in your eyes?

DAY 2 SUMMARY

- Church is much more that a place to go on Sundays; it is the doorway through which you can do the good works God has prepared for you.
- Joining a new church when you leave home signifies that you are spiritually well-prepared for your future.

Write your own prayer here.

_____

_____

_____

_____

DAY 3: MADE FOR MINISTRY

Read the words to this song and then review the memory passage for the week.

'Cause we are a family whose hearts are blazing
So let's raise our candles and light up the sky
Prayin' to our Father "In the Name of Jesus
Make us a beacon in darkest times."

So carry your candle and run to the darkness
Seek out the hopeless, deceived and poor
And hold out your candle for all to see it
Take your candle and go light your world
Take your candle and go light your world[1]

Matthew 5:14-16

_____

_____

_____

_____

_____

_____

God ordained you to shine light into a spiritually dark world. You are a lamp, and the church is your lampstand. Many high school students sit passively and allow the church to meet their needs. But according to God's Word, you are involved in His plan to reach the world for Christ.

Write 2 Corinthians 5:20 below.

_____

_____

_____

When the president needs a person to represent the United States abroad, he calls an ambassador. The ambassador's role is to stand in place of the president. You are Christ's ambassador; among your friends and family, you

[1] Chris Rice, "The Candle Song" (BMG Songs, Inc., 1993).

represent the Kingdom of Heaven. You stand in place of Jesus Christ. What an awesome responsibility!

Look back at 2 Corinthians 5:20. Circle the phrase which follows the word "ambassador."

God wants the people you know to come to know Him. He could show up in their bedroom one night, or send them a telegram from heaven. But instead, God chooses to make His appeal through you. Therefore, if you choose not to speak or act on Christ's behalf, how will God make His desire known to them?

"Wait a minute," you might be thinking. "I'm not mature enough to speak on behalf of God. The church has professional people to do that."

Read Ephesians 4:11-13 below.

It was he who gave some to be apostles, some to be prophets, some to be evangelists, and some to be pastors and teachers, to prepare God's people for works of service, so that the body of Christ may be built up until we all reach unity in the faith and in the knowledge of the Son of God and become mature, attaining to the whole measure of the fullness of Christ.

What five ministry roles are mentioned?

1. _____

2. _____

3. _____

4. _____

5. _____

These are some of the wonderful functions God provides through the Body of Christ. Apostles start new churches. Prophets stand against the current of society, calling believers to swim upstream. Evangelists lead non-Christians to saving faith. Pastors shepherd young believers into maturity. Teachers ensure that God's Word remains central in the life and function of the church.

But take a second look at Ephesians 4. What are the people in these roles supposed to do?

❑ lead the church ❑ works of service
❑ pray for others ❑ prepare and equip others

God makes His appeal through you!

You may think ministry is only for the trained professionals. Not true! Professional clergy members have this holy task: to prepare God's people for works of service. God wants you in His service. He will utilize ministers to help you prepare.

You take a major step toward Christian maturity when the church stops trying to evangelize you, and you begin to help the church reach others. Recall from Week Six, participating in ministry is a "meat" activity that goes beyond an infant's need for milk.

Picturing yourself as a minister may be a radically new concept for you. You possibly feel unprepared and unskilled. According to Scripture, when you received God's Sprit at the time of salvation, He also equipped you for ministry. God gave you spiritual gifts to build the church. In case you haven't studied the various spiritual gifts mentioned in the Bible, identify them by completing this next activity.

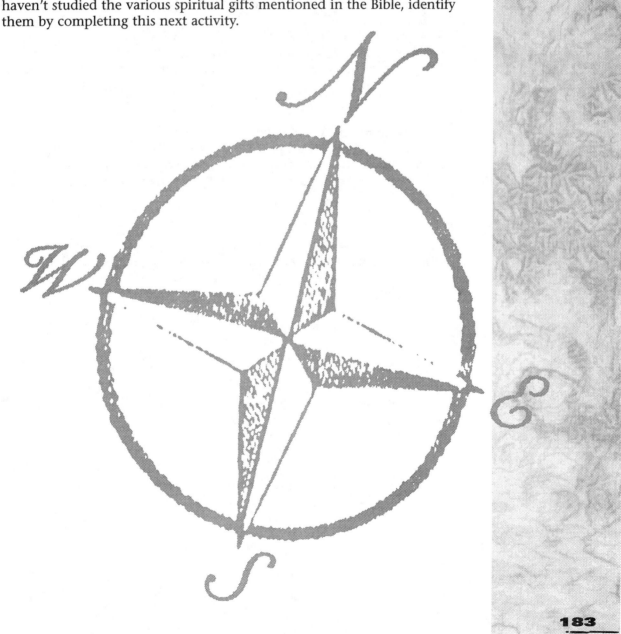

Read the passages below and record the spiritual gifts in the margin. The list has already been started with the five gifts listed from Ephesians 4. Some gifts are mentioned in more than one passage, but only record each gift once.

1. Apostleship

2. Prophecy

3. Evangelism

4. Pastoring

5. Teaching

6.

7.

8.

9.

10.

11.

12.

13.

14.

15.

16.

17.

18.

19.

20.

Ephesians 4:11-13 *It was he who gave some to be **apostles**, some to be **prophets**, some to be **evangelists**, and some to be **pastors** and **teachers**, to prepare God's people for works of service, so that the body of Christ may be built up until we all reach unity in the faith and in the knowledge of the Son of God and become mature, attaining to the whole measure of the fullness of Christ.*

1 Corinthians 12:8-10 *To one there is given through the Spirit the message of **wisdom**, to another the message of **knowledge** by means of the same Spirit, to another **faith** by the same Spirit, to another gifts of **healing**, by that one Spirit, to another **miraculous powers**, to another prophecy, to another **distinguishing between spirits (discernment)**, to another speaking in different kinds of **tongues**, and to still another the **interpretation** of tongues.*

1 Corinthians 12:28 *And in the church God has appointed first of all apostles, second prophets, third teachers, then workers of miracles, also those having gifts of healing, those able to **help [service]** others, those with gifts of **administration**, and those speaking in different kinds of tongues.*

Romans 12:6-8 *We have different gifts, according to the grace given us. If a man's gift is prophesying, let him use it in proportion to his faith. If it is serving, let him serve; if it is teaching, let him teach; if it is **encouraging**, let him encourage; if it is **contributing [giving]** to the needs of others, let him give generously; if it is **leadership**, let him govern diligently; if it is showing **mercy**, let him do it cheerfully.*

1 Peter 4:9-10 *Offer **hospitality** to one another without grumbling. Each one should use whatever gift he has received to serve others., faithfully administering God's grace in its various forms.*

Churches and denominations understand the list of gifts differently. Some teach that fewer gifts are given today. Some churches add other gifts alluded to in Scripture. Whatever your church's specific teachings about spiritual gifts, the point in this study is for you to see that God gives them to His followers.

Read 1 Corinthians 12: 7, 11.

According to these verses, to whom are these gifts given?

❑ mature believers   ❑ professional ministers
❑ each one   ❑ seminary graduates

It is easy for a high school senior to feel inadequate as a leader in ministry. But as you can see by the list, spiritual gifts come in a wide variety. You may use your gifts every week in church and never teach a Bible study to a group. God's purpose is clear: He wants to build the church through you. Your youth group probably includes students from seventh through 12th grades. Why don't you find a way to help a younger student grow in faith? Ask your youth minister if he or she has some ideas for you to begin contributing to the growth of someone else in the group. He or she may know some other area of service in the church that needs someone just like you.

Think of several ways you can begin to participate in the ministry of the church as a high school senior. Record your ideas in the box below and then use it as a guideline for application.

> *Become a part of your church's ministry.*

Ministry is not reserved for the professionally trained; it is for divinely gifted ambassadors. Let God make His appeal to others through you.

DAY 3 SUMMARY

- You are Christ's ambassador to the world.
- God has gifted you in order to build the church.

Write your prayer here.

_____

_____

_____

_____

_____

DAY 4: A SERVANT'S HEART

Begin today's study by praying for God to reveal Himself to you. He has been looking forward to this meeting with you. Remain mindful of His presence as you move through the lesson.

Write out this week's memory passage—from memory, if you can.

Matthew 5:14-16

_____

_____

_____

_____

_____

_____

What is a practical way to let your light shine for Christ today?

```
┌─────────────────────────────────────────────┐
│                                               │
│                                               │
│                                               │
│                                               │
└─────────────────────────────────────────────┘
```

You can see the end of the road for this workbook. Tomorrow you will choose some specific points of application to put into practice.

This week you have learned that the time you spend alone with God transforms into time you spend building the church. In other words, ingestion (feeding on God) leads to digestion (application) which leads to expressions of your faith in service to others. As a final Bible study today, you will examine the perfect biblical model of servanthood.

Who are some famous people considered great in this world? (athletes, celebrities, etc.)

```
┌─────────────────────────────────────────────┐
│                                               │
│                                               │
│                                               │
│                                               │
└─────────────────────────────────────────────┘
```

Ingest then digest!

Read Matthew 20:20-28.

Who came with a request to Jesus?

_____

On whose behalf was she making this request?

_____

What did they want?

❑ to sit with Jesus   ❑ recognition as great
❑ positions of power   ❑ all of the above

James and John wanted it all! They knew that Jesus was God in the flesh, and they believed He would reign on an everlasting throne. Kings and rulers put the most powerful leaders on either side of the throne. These two men were asking to be exalted (lifted up) above all other humans to these positions of greatness.

How did the other ten disciples react to James and John's request?

_____

_____

If you combine the words jealous, angry, and disgusted you get the word indignant. This reaction often happens when one person is exalted above another. Battles for position, power, and prestige rage daily in the work force. And in the classroom, students war over grades, scholarships, and academic honors. In the end, many people define greatness as achieving status.

Indignant = anger aroused by injustice.

Record Jesus' opinion on this quest for status and power as stated in the first phrase of verse 26.

_____

_____

Jesus redefines what it means to be great. Write the rest of verse 26 below:

_____

_____

Go back to the thought box where you listed great people. Circle the ones— if any—who became great through servanthood.

If anyone had a right to claim greatness and thus seize control of all things, it was Jesus. He existed with God before the creation of the world (John 1:1-3). He was the visible image of the invisible God (Colossians 1:15). All the fullness of God dwelled in Jesus (Colossians 1:19). He was known for His eternal riches (2 Corinthians 8:9). He rose from the grave and now sits on the throne of heaven (Hebrews 12:2). Scripture says that at His name, every knee will bow and every tongue will confess that He is the Lord (Philippians 2:10-11).

Jesus, however, chose to express His greatness in an unusual way.

According to Matthew 20:28, why did Jesus come to the earth?

❑ to give his life   ❑ to be a ransom
❑ to serve   ❑ to be served

The King of Glory—the One who will be worshiped eternally and the One who listens to your heart as you read this page—came to serve others.

Now, wrestle with this question for a minute:

If Jesus came to serve others, what are you doing with your time?

During Week Two you learned that God's will for your life is for you to be conformed to the image of Jesus. Maybe you thought the image of Jesus was as a leader or a famously wealthy famous figure. The truth is that you are to be conformed to His image as a servant.

Read each of the following passages to get a wider understanding of what the Bible says about servanthood.

Galatians 5:13

1 Peter 4:10-11

Ephesians 6:7-8

Romans 14:17-18

How can you summarize these verses as a practical application point for your life?

_____

_____

Nothing brings you into closer identification with Christ than to serve others. He came to show you the way to greatness in the eyes of God. As you approach graduation, resolve now to be a spiritual leader by imitating Jesus as a servant.

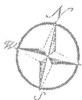

DAY 4 SUMMARY

- Jesus defined greatness by choosing to serve.
- You are to be conformed to His image as a servant of others.

Write your own prayer here.

_____

_____

_____

_____

_____

DAY 5: THE EXPEDITION

Congratulations! You made it to the very end of the trail. Today you will sit on "top" of this mountainous study and look back on your journey.

You see, in truth, your expedition is only about to begin. Graduation is the doorway to the rest of your life. Hopefully this study has helped prepare you for the new adventures in your future. But don't wait until you walk out the door of your parent's home for good to apply the lessons you have been learning over the past eight weeks. The more you practice taking responsibility for your own spiritual growth now, the better prepared you will be when you are really on your own. Use the worksheet below to help you review and process what you have learned along the way. By the end you should identify at least three things you can put into daily practice in the present.

Flip back to Week One. Write the memory verse in the blanks that follow. (Try to actually do it from memory!) Then read the summary statements and look for two or three points that stood out to you from the whole week. Record those on the following page.

WEEK ONE:
SOCIAL SECURITY

Ephesians 1:11-12

_____

_____

_____

_____

_____

_____

_____

_____

The most important lessons I learned are:

- _____

  _____

  _____

- _____

  _____

  _____

- _____

  _____

  _____

Repeat these same steps for each week.

WEEK TWO:
WHERE THERE'S A WORD, THERE'S A WILL

Jeremiah 29:11-13

_____

_____

_____

_____

_____

_____

_____

_____

The most important lessons I learned are:

- _____

  _____

  _____

- _____

  _____

  _____

- _____

  _____

  _____

WEEK THREE:
WHERE THERE'S A WILL, THERE'S A WAY

Psalm 24:4-5

_____

_____

_____

_____

_____

_____

_____

_____

The most important lessons I learned are:

• _____

_____

_____

• _____

_____

_____

• _____

_____

_____

WEEK FOUR:
THE DATING GAME

Ephesians 5:31-32

_____

_____

_____

_____

_____

_____

_____

_____

The most important lessons I learned are:

- _____

_____

_____

_____

- _____

_____

_____

- _____

_____

_____

WEEK FIVE: HOME FREE

Malachi 1:6

_____

_____

_____

_____

_____

_____

_____

_____

The most important lessons I learned are:

- _____

_____

_____

- _____

_____

_____

- _____

_____

_____

WEEK SIX:
THE ROAD OF SPIRITUAL GROWTH

Hebrews 5:13-14

_____

_____

_____

_____

_____

_____

_____

_____

The most important lessons I learned are:

- _____

_____

_____

- _____

_____

_____

- _____

_____

_____

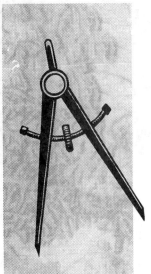

WEEK SEVEN:
SPIRITUAL FITNESS — DIET

Hebrews 11:6

_____

_____

_____

_____

_____

_____

_____

_____

The most important lessons I learned are:

- _____

_____

_____

- _____

_____

_____

- _____

_____

_____

WEEK EIGHT:
SPIRITUAL FITNESS — EXERCISE

Matthew 5:14-16

_____

_____

_____

_____

_____

_____

_____

_____

The most important lessons I learned are:

- _____

  _____

  _____

- _____

  _____

  _____

- _____

  _____

  _____

In this exercise you have compiled the most valuable words of God to you during this study. Remember James 1:22 which says, "Do not merely listen to the word, and so deceive yourselves. Do what it says."

Of all the important lessons you have learned, pick three to write down as personal applications. Make these applications useful for the time you still have at home.

APPLICATION POINT #1

By God's strength and power, I will

_____

_____

APPLICATION POINT #2

By God's strength and power, I will

_____

_____

APPLICATION POINT #3

By God's strength and power, I will

_____

_____

Statistically, by this time next year you probably would have dropped out of the spiritual race. But since you made it to the end of this workbook, surely you can make it spiritually next year also.

God no longer walks in the Garden of Eden. He prefers to walk with you. Get up tomorrow and meet Him again.

And enjoy the journey!

200